Island Alliance Church
510 Thompson Creek Road
Stevensville, MD 21666

We Let
Our Son Die

We Let Our Son Die

by Larry Parker

as told to Don Tanner

234.2

Harvest House Publishers
Irvine, California 92714

Quotations from the Bible have been taken from the New American Standard version, copyright © The Lockman Foundation 1960, 1962, 1963, 1968, 1971, 1972, 1973, 1975, used by permission; and the Authorized King James version. The names of many in this book have been changed to protect their privacy.

TO
our beloved son
Wesley
May his death
not be in vain

Acknowledgments

To my wife, Lucky, who is as much the author of this book as I. To Harald Bredesen, Annamae Cheney, and Bob Slosser for their encouragement to write our story. To Don Tanner and his lovely wife, Sally, who became our dear friends, and without whose counsel and writing this book could not have been possible. To Jim Schooler, for his sensitivity and writing skills in helping Don develop this manuscript.

To Pastor Gary Nash for his cooperation and contribution to this book. To Dick and Betty Mills, whose ministry to us proved to be a turning point in our lives. To the many persons across the country whose letters of encouragement and prayers enabled us to survive and learn from this terrible ordeal.

—Larry Parker

Foreword

This book is a success story.

It took great courage for Larry and Lucky Parker to relive their agony. Yet because of the sacrificial love of this couple, many parents will be spared the heartache of a presumptive leap in the dark.

Vindictive critics may wish that the Parkers had fallen in defeat. But God had other plans. Larry and Lucky reflect the courage of Micah when he wrote, "Rejoice not against me, O mine enemy: When I fall, I shall rise; when I sit in darkness, the Lord shall be a light unto me" (Micah 7:8).

Most couples would have been destroyed by the emotional, mental, physical, spiritual, and financial stress they suffered. But, as a "just man falls seven times and rises again" (Proverbs 24:16), the Parkers endured, rose from defeat, and lived—victoriously.

This book is a success story, not only because it portrays the personal triumph of the Parkers, but because it will help scores of believers avoid the pitfalls of presumption and lead them into a balanced view of faith.

—Dick Mills

Contents

1

Into the Lion's Den

The opening elevator door triggered a flurry of activity. A wall of television cameras began to whir, their huge blinding lights stabbing the shadows from the hallway amid bursts of flashbulbs and strobes. Reporters from major newspapers, the international wire services, national magazines, television and radio stations clogged the narrow corridor. Lucky and I had attracted the attention of the world.

Blinking from surprise and from the heavy glare, we hurriedly stepped down the hall to the courtroom. Arm in arm, clutching our Bibles like Daniels heading for a lion's den, we were ready to face charges of involuntary manslaughter and felony child abuse. Our lawyers had told us that this case was big, but we didn't know how big. All we knew was that our eleven-year-old diabetic son, Wesley, had died because we wanted to believe that he was healed and didn't need his insulin injections anymore. We had stood on our faith, but somewhere, somehow, something had gone wrong.

"Mr. and Mrs. Parker, is it true that you killed your diabetic son by denying him insulin?" a reporter asked callously.

My stomach turned, and Lucky's eyes flashed with hurt and fear. The advice of my attorney, Bill Russler, quickly crossed my mind: "Don't say *anything* to the media, not even 'No comment.'" We had been abused and misquoted by the press so many times that we didn't trust them. We felt prejudged and that anything we said would be used against us.

I hurriedly pulled Lucky away from the newsman and through the door into the courtroom. As she looked up at me, terror blazed through her eyes.

"Oh, God, help my wife," I breathed.

Leaving the noisy clamor of the newsmedia, we marched through the relative peace of the gallery to the railing that separated it from the court and sat down. As we waited in the quiet, I had a sense of floating above the scene, observing objectively the reactions of the people around us. Some eyes and heads turned away in shame, others glared at us despicably, a few softened with pity. Finally, Lucky's lawyer entered the courtroom. Noticing where we were sitting, Lee Simmons strode toward us.

"Hello, Lucky, Larry . . . How are you feeling this morning? Fine? Good. We have a big day ahead of us. In fact . . . please come over to the other side of the railing."

We rose slowly from our gallery seats, crossed through the gate in the railing to the table in the middle of the courtoom and sat down. I noticed how similar our surroundings were to the courtrooms I had seen in movies on television, and the one in Barstow, California, where I served as the foreman of a jury during another trial. The empty jury box was to our right, and slightly to the left the judge's bench was elevated in front of us. The court recorder was positioned between the bench and the witness stand. Scanning the room, my eyes met the stare of the bailiff, standing with crossed arms at my left. The prosecutor, Tom Frazier, and our lawyers began setting up their briefcases and arranging their papers on the table that we shared, the prosecutor on our right, Lucky and I with our attorneys on the left. Instinctively, we wanted to move far to the left to put as much distance between us and Frazier as possible.

The gallery was filling with spectators. I noticed that some were prospective jurors who were not selected. Others were people who worked in the courthouse, and some were from the media. As if on cue a door opened to the right of the witness stand, and twelve men and women stepped into the jury box and sat down. We felt like animals on display in a zoo.

When everyone was seated, Judge J. Steve Williams emerged through a private entry, stepped up to the bench, sat down, and nodded toward the bailiff.

"Court is now in order," the bailiff announced loudly.

"Good morning, ladies and gentlemen," the judge smiled at the jurors. He turned to face our table and the gallery behind us. "The record will reflect that the jurors are all present and in their places; also the alternate jurors. The defendants are present with Counsel. At this time the clerk will swear the alternate jurors. Will they please stand and raise their right hands to be sworn . . . ."

Simmons leaned over and whispered, "Judge Williams is a good judge. We're 'lucky' to have him." Lucky and I smiled faintly. I observed the judge closely and agreed. When this big man with graying hair and long black robe strode into position, we sensed kindness radiating from his eyes. Immediately we felt reassured that whatever the outcome of the trial, surely he would be just.

With the alternates sworn, Judge Williams again turned to the jury. There was a stirring in the gallery—the real courtroom drama was about to begin.

"Ladies and gentlemen of the jury, we are about to commence with the opening statements made by Counsel," the judge instructed. "The purpose of an opening statement is to, in effect, furnish a road map of how the evidence will perhaps unfold during the course of the trial."

"You should bear in mind that the statements of Counsel are not evidence, and everything that is said during the course of an opening statement might be prefaced by, 'We intend to prove' or 'We expect the evidence will show.' Your responsibility is going to be to determine just what, in fact, the evidence does establish . . . ."

As Judge Williams continued his instructions, I followed Lucky's gaze to the Great Seal of the State of California, set into the wall above the bench. I was relieved to see that the panic evident in her facial expression before had been replaced with a look of interest and calm.

Fixing my stare on the Seal, I sincerely believed in the American judicial system. My fear dissipated some, and I was eager to see how justice would operate in our case. I wanted to reach over and pat Lucky's folded hands, which were resting on the top of the table, but that was impossible because our attorneys sat between us. We looked at each other instead, and smiled.

"At this time you may proceed, Mr. Frazier, with your opening statement."

The judge nodded toward the prosecutor; he stood

and approached the jury box. Crossing the room, Frazier looked back at the Counselors' table, glared at Lucky and me for a second, then turned and stopped in front of the jury.

"Ladies and gentlemen of the jury, . . ." he began pompously.

Intrigued by the proceeding, I listened intently to Frazier's argument, storing in my mind what he thought to be significant points. As Lucky's attorney offered his opening statement in our defense, I mentally did the same thing. *It will be interesting,* I mused, *to see how this whole thing lines up.* Throughout the proceedings, Lucky continued her stare at the Seal, praying silently and concentrating on the contents of the emblem to block out the hurtful oratory of the prosecutor as he probed into sensitive areas.

The opening remarks took the rest of the morning. As Lucky and I walked out of the courtroom and into the hall during the lunch recess, we were acutely aware of reporters crowding around us like impatient vultures. We hurried past them for the refuge of the elevator. Outside, we strolled down the walk toward a sundial, our eyes stinging from the heavy San Bernardino smog. The air was thick and muggy—a far cry from the beautiful spring morning we had enjoyed earlier as we stepped out of our car in the County Courthouse parking lot.

I loved the spring! I recalled how the sun was shining brightly through fleecy clouds earlier in the day as the morning pressed itself against my face. Like so many times before, I felt assured that God was on our side. I leaned into the car, picked up my Bible off the front seat, stepped back and shut the door, then peered over the roof of the car at Lucky. She slammed her door, and quickly glanced up, a nervous smile flickering across her face. She was clutching her Bible as if it were a much loved doll.

"Let's go, honey," I nodded.

"Oh, Larry, I'm so nervous," she whispered, stepping around the car to join me. I grasped her hand tightly during the short walk to the court building, trying to comfort her. She looked beautiful, dressed in a green dress and white sweater with yellow, salmon and turquoise embroidered flowers.

"Just remember Romans 8:28: '*All* things work together for good to them that love God . . . .' Remember it. That's our promise, Lucky."

We looked up to the third floor of the six-story building where our trial was to be held. At that moment I needed all the promises from God that we could get. The sight of the double glass doors of the building sent a wave of fear through me as we opened them and walked into the cool, well-lit corridor, its walls and floors shining as if they had been carefully polished. I pressed the elevator button and waited. Several others joined us for the wait, obviously people who worked in the building. We were soon enveloped by the embarrassed silence that usually accompanies elevator rides. The shuffling, tapping feet, checking of wristwatches, staring at the elevator ceiling, door or floor, yawning occasionally, the nonchalant attitude of persons just arriving for work—these gave me clues as to who these people were as we rode to the third floor. I was hoping that no one would recognize us.

Lucky was clutching my hand so tightly that her knuckles were white. She had the look of a frightened kitten. I squeezed, and she looked up. That nervous smile flickered across her face once more.

"Everything's going to be all right," I reassured.

"I know . . . thank you, honey," she whispered back . . . .

As we returned to the courtroom after the noon recess, we wondered how the attorneys would defend us. The gallery filled again with spectators, and court was called to order. Soon the excitement wore off as the trial fell into a routine of questions and answers for the witnesses.

The first to be called was Ralph Braun, my former biology professor at Barstow College. I had written a term paper on diabetes for his class the summer before. Why had he been called? It soon became apparent that Frazier intended to show that I knew the consequences of holding back Wesley's insulin.

"You may call your next witness, Mr. Frazier."

"Thank you, Your Honor. Call Dr. Robert Chinnock."

Wesley's physician stood from the gallery and stepped spryly to the witness stand. Although he was an elderly man, his mind was as sharp and keen as a scalpel.

"Dr. Chinnock, tell us about your educational background, please."

He answered in his crisp, clipped style: "Finished Loma Linda University School of Medicine in 1943; internship and residency at White Memorial Hospital in Los Angeles, '43 to '45; and further residency at State University of Iowa Hospital, '45 to '47."

"And did you have an area of specialty that you studied?"

"Graduate training was in the field of pediatrics." Dr. Chinnock's demeanor was still and became more so as he was questioned further.

"And have you been involved in the practice of medicine since 1947?"

"I have been in the practice of medicine following my graduate training completed in 1948."

"And is there any area within the field of pediatrics that you have a specialty in?"

"One of my areas of special interest has been diabetes in children."

Mr. Frazier turned slightly to look toward the Counselors' table. "And with regard to that, do you know Mr. and Mrs. Parker?"

I leaned forward and listened intently. What began as a set of meaningless questions was assuming an ominous direction.

"Yes, I do." Nervousness was betrayed in Dr. Chinnock's voice as he glanced at us. A slight hurt look crept across his face. Had we offended him by the action that we had taken with Wesley? Was he for us? Our relationship had always been very cordial. He was a man full of compassion, warmth and genuine friendliness. I prayed silently that we had not hurt him.

Frazier continued, "Do you recognize them in the courtroom?"

"Yes, I do."

"Could you point them out for us?"

Dr. Chinnock lifted his right hand to point at us. It trembled slightly. The pain on his face was even more evident.

"Could the record reflect that the witness has identified the defendants?"

"The record will so reflect," Judge Williams intoned.

Frazier turned back to the doctor and resumed his

questioning: "Can you tell us, doctor, how your knowledge or acquaintance with the Parkers came about?"

"My first contact with them, as I recall, was when their son, Wesley, was transferred to the Loma Linda University Hospital because of some problems he was having with his diabetes at that time . . . ."

I remembered. It was February 1972. Lucky was stirring pudding in the kitchen when the front screen door slammed, announcing the arrival of our children home from school.

"Hi, Mom!" Pam greeted cheerfully, disappearing down the hall to her bedroom.

Lucky waited for Wess to follow, then became curious.

"Pam, where's Wess?" she called loudly.

"He's in the living room, Mom."

"Wesley, go change your clothes."

Silence.

"Wess, answer me! Pam, is Wess all right?"

"Yeah, I guess so," her voice grew louder as she emerged from the hall. "Mom!"

Alarmed, Lucky quickly turned off the stove and rushed into the living room. "Pam, go get Bobby next door. Ask him to come quickly and help me get Wess into the car. Hurry!"

Lucky drove Wesley to Barstow Community Hospital and then called me. I returned home from work just in time to pick up our other children and follow the ambulance to Loma Linda Hospital.

We had made an appointment with Dr. Chinnock after Wesley's first doctor died. This emergency arose before we could see him. Under Dr. Chinnock's care,

Wess was back to his old self within a day or so. We felt indebted to this specialist after that, and were impressed enough to make him Wesley's physician. We appreciated him for teaching us how to keep Wesley's diet better balanced to minimize insulin reaction and what to do in case of an emergency.

". . . And was there a diagnosis as to his problem at the time that you saw him?" Frazier asked Dr. Chinnock.

"The diagnosis of his problem was that of diabetes mellitus, with a low blood sugar reaction at that time."

"And as a result of the condition that you found Wesley in, did you prescribe any medication or take steps to remedy the situation?"

"He was given intravenous fluids on admission, and he was given some feeding and responded well to this."

"When you say 'feeding' is this normal . . . ?"

"Food . . . ."

"And was he in the hospital for some time after being admitted?"

"From February 16 to February 23, 1972."

"Any time during that period, did you have conversations with Mr. and Mrs. Parker with regard to Wesley's condition?"

Again Dr. Chinnock glanced at us. The hurt on his face was mixed with compassion. Perhaps he was remembering that conversation we had with him, which was probably typical for parents of a diabetic child. We were on the verge of panic. But his assurances relieved many of our fears and frustrations. We learned then that Wesley should have been taking another form of insulin, which the hospital began administering to him immediately. His condition improved tremendously after that.

Dr. Chinnock answered the prosecutor. "Yes, I did. As is my custom with all families and young people with diabetes when I first see the parents, we usually spend several sessions talking about the disease, its basic background, the aspects of regulation, and the things that are necessary for these young people to live as normal a life as possible."

Frazier folded his arms and cocked his head in interest. "Based on your experience and training, can you tell us how diabetes comes about?"

Dr. Chinnock's face and voice brightened at this point. "Diabetes in children results from the inability of the small cells of the pancreas gland to produce adequate amounts of insulin and . . . ."

I looked around the courtroom at this point and noted the tell-tale signs of waning interest among the spectators—a few stifled yawns, sporatic whispering, some glazed stares toward the witness stand. These reactions angered me—how could people and the press determine what was happening if they didn't understand the disease?

Still happily sharing his knowledge with the court, Dr. Chinnock explained the physiological problems associated with diabetes. Soon even I was beginning to associate myself with the gallery—having heard this lecture before, several times.

The pancreas delivers insulin on demand from the body, which is used to lower the sugar level in the blood by converting it to energy. Life for a total diabetic child such as Wesley was like a razor edge of terror. Diet, insulin, and physical exertion must be balanced correctly to avoid diabetic coma or hypoglycemia.

With *too little* insulin, blood sugar would be high, bringing frequent urination and loss of strength. Pain in the joints, head, and stomach would come next, followed by diabetic coma then death. On the other hand, *too much* insulin would result in hypoglycemia or low blood sugar. The resulting insulin reaction can come suddenly. Wesley would become pale and unable to react to his surroundings. Unconsciousness and death would follow if sugar was not supplied for his blood immediately. Only the parents of a total diabetic can understand the horror and helplessness of insulin reaction.

I recalled one such incident. Wess had come home from school one afternoon looking pale. I put a teaspoon of sugar into a glass of milk and offered it to him. Sitting on a chair by the dining room table with a glassy stare in his eyes, he refused.

"Drink it, Wesley!"

He didn't move.

"Wesley! Drink the milk!" I shouted, trying to break through his increasingly foggy mind.

Tilting his head back, I poured the liquid between his lips. He brushed his hand at the glass, knocking it to the floor where it shattered, spilling the milk across the room. I picked Wess up and carried him to the couch in the living room.

"Lucky! Make up another glass."

Wesley was fighting me now as his body thrashed out aimlessly in reaction to his sugar starved blood.

"Hurry, Lucky. Hurry!"

I held him down and forced his mouth open while Lucky tried to pour some of the sugar treated milk into him.

"Please, son, you've got to drink!" We pleaded.

"Oh, God, help us!"

Milk poured all over Wesley's face, us, and the

couch. Somehow some of it must have gotten down his throat. After what seemed an eternity of anguish, Wesley began to calm down.

"Oh . . . oh . . . my head . . . hurts," he moaned.

Frazier's next question took a different turn. "Now were you involved in any type of summer program for diabetics?"

"Since 1958 I have been in charge of a summer camp program for children with diabetes, sponsored by the Diabetes Association of Southern California."

"Can you tell us where that takes place and what it involves?"

"It is essentially a two-week session in the San Bernardino mountains where there is opportunity for them to engage in normal summer camp activity in a controlled environment."

"And did Wesley participate in this camp?"

"Yes, he was in camp last summer."

Wesley at summer camp! I smiled at my brief recollection of his excited, smiling face as he hopped off the camp bus and ran into our arms at Loma Linda University, where the campers were picked up and dropped off.

"Boy, that was the best time!" he proclaimed loudly.

He hugged his mom tightly and grinned, "I had a good time, but I missed you a whole lot." Lucky was laughing and gasping.

"Wess, don't squeeze me so tightly . . . I can't breathe!"

Wesley had a lot of sensitivity for an eleven-year-old.

My mind drifted back to the courtroom discussion. Remembering that sobering thought about Wess helped me focus on Frazier's next question to Dr. Chinnock.

"Did Wesley appear to have a grasp of the nature of his illness?"

"I assume that he did because it is my custom to involve the young person with the family as we talk about diabetes."

"Doctor, is it your opinion that Wesley would always need insulin?"

Lucky and I stiffened at this question. We knew what the doctor would say. He had told us many times that diabetes is not an illness or disease, but a "way of life". This line of questioning was leading to only one conclusion—that Wesley could never have been cured of diabetes.

"Yes," Dr. Chinnock answered quickly.

"How would you classify him as a diabetic; would you call him a total . . .?"

"If you wish to use that term 'total diabetic,' yes. Total diabetes refers to the time when the body no longer manufactures insulin. The majority of young people with diabetes will become total diabetics within a matter of five or six years."

"How long have you been treating diabetics?"

"During my whole professional career."

"Have you at any time ever found a total diabetic like Wesley who no longer needed insulin?"

"I have not."

Frazier turned abruptly and glanced at the Counselors' table. Dr. Chinnock blinked in surprise at the sudden reaction of the prosecutor. Regaining his composure, the physician turned his head slightly and gazed sadly at us. The hurt look on his face vanished. All that remained was pity. The prosecutor had made his point.

Frazier turned slowly to face the doctor. He resumed his questioning, but my mind was miles away, swirling in the confusion of the moment.

They were saying that our son could never have been healed. But God *does* heal—I had seen it! Cancer, shattered bones, blasted minds, touched by the power of God. How dare they say that my God could not cure a person of diabetes!

Doubt, pain, anger, resentment—the floodgates of my heart opened, pouring these ugly emotions into my being. How I cried out for Wesley.

The session droned late into the afternoon, and I dreaded the long, hot drive home through the desert. Later as the car sped through the barren land toward Barstow, memories of the past brought stinging tears to my eyes. For a moment I blamed my watering eyes on the smog, but that thought passed as I drifted back to the day when the nightmare began.

2

"I'm Healed!"

The evangelist took Wesley firmly by the shoulders and drew him close.

"Wesley, do you know the Lord Jesus as your Savior?"

"Yes."

"Do you believe that God loves you?"

"Yes."

"Do you love God?"

"Yes. . . ."

Tears welled in Wesley's eyes, and one finally rolled down his cheek as he lifted his face to look the minister in the eyes.

"Do you understand what we are going to pray for now?"

"Yes. I want to be healed of diabetes."

"I believe God is going to heal you, Wesley. Do you believe it?"

"Uh huh."

"Raise your hands, and praise God for it."

The evangelist smiled warmly. "Brother and Sister Parker, could you join me in prayer now?"

Reverend Dan Romero laid his hands on Wesley's head and Lucky and I, with Wess between us, placed our arms around our son. I momentarily touched Lucky's shoulder.

She looked at me with tears of hope and anticipation

in her eyes, and opened her mouth slightly. "Oh, Jesus . . . ." she whispered.

Lucky closed her eyes, forcing several tears to trickle down her face. A loud "hallelujah" rang out at that moment to our right. Startled from my concentration in prayer, I glanced at a heavy-set older woman in a flower-print dress lifting her arms as she knelt, her face covered by an expression of rapture. Pastor Gary Nash was looking down at her, his arms raised in like manner, smiling.

Praise God, I thought. *She's really been touched by the Lord.* I turned to face the young evangelist and closed my eyes. That woman's joyful face encouraged me. *Maybe Wess will be healed today. Maybe this is the time.*

"Father, we bring Wesley before you in Jesus' name," Romero prayed fervently. "Because your Word says that whenever 'two shall agree on earth as touching any thing . . . it shall be done,' and that 'by His stripes you *were* healed,' we believe by these Scriptures that you will heal. We receive it by faith, Lord. In Jesus' name we pray. Amen."

Wesley grinned in child-like acceptance. Feeling a strong emotion of love pulse through my body toward Wess, I was glad that we had brought him up to the altar for prayer. . . .

I was feeling good that day. It was a typically beautiful, hot summer's day on the desert. Lucky looked radiant in her pink dress, and Wesley had the appearance of a little gentleman in his slacks, white shirt and tie. The girls were like princesses in their bright summer outfits. As Lucky and I rounded up the kids and herded them into our tan 1962 Dodge for the drive to church, I thought of how good God had been to us. Laid off from my technician's job at the Goldstone Tracking Station, I looked forward with excitement to see how He was going to provide for our needs. He had demonstrated His ability to take care of us so many times before! What form would His provision take this time?

As we drove the three short miles to church, the conversation in the car kept turning to this subject: "The Lord will provide, He will see us through . . . ."

We took the children to children's church and Lucky and I headed for the sanctuary.

"Good morning, Larry, Hi, Lucky . . . Praise God for this beautiful day, eh?" Pastor Nash greeted as we approached.

"Morning, Pastor," Lucky smiled, breezing past and into the building to find seats. I stopped to talk.

"Morning, Brother Nash," I greeted cheerfully. "So, is our evangelist going to be speaking today?" I knew from the previous Sunday's bulletin that we were supposed to have a guest preacher.

"Yes, yes!" Pastor Nash seemed excited as he told me how Romero had been laid up in the Barstow hospital all week with a painful spine condition and had cancelled his engagement. Then on Saturday, he had called and said that he would be coming afterall, that God had healed his back. Knowing something miraculous had happened to our speaker made me feel even better. I looked forward to the service with a growing expectancy.

"I thank you all for praying for me last week," the evangelist began as he greeted the congregation. He stood on the stage in the front of the sanctuary, in full view of the audience. The auditorium was almost full. *More people than last Sunday*, I mused.

"I know that it was because of your prayers for me that I'm here today, healed, and feeling better than I have for a long time. As you probably already know, I have a spine condition. I mean *had*," he smiled broadly. ". . . I couldn't even bend over. Now look . . . ."

Romero demonstrated his new mobility by touching his toes once, twice, three times. Then he stretched his arms high above his head, looked out over the congregation and yelled, "Hallelujah! Hallelujah . . . ." I said, "Hallelujah!"

The audience responded with hearty applause, giving God the glory for the wonderful miracle. As the staccato thunder of the clapping died, Romero strode to the preacher's podium in the middle of the stage, opened his Bible, thumbed over a few pages, and placed his hands on the sides of the pulpit as he gazed at us. He looked down again, and began to read:

"In the book of the Revelation, chapter twenty, verse eleven. . . ." Romero paused for a moment, listening to the rustle of pages being turned as the people searched for his text.

". . . It says, 'And I saw a great white throne, and Him that sat on it, from whose face the earth and the heaven fled away; and there was found no place for them. And I saw the dead, small and great, stand before God; and the books were opened: and another book was opened, which is the book of life: and the dead were judged out of those things which were written in the books, according to their works. And the sea gave up the dead which were in it; and death and hell delivered up the dead which were in them: and they were judged every man according to their works. And death and hell were cast into the lake of fire. This is the second death. And whosoever was not found written in the Book of Life was cast into the lake of fire.' "

Slowly the evangelist closed his Bible, eyes still looking down. Tension mounted. Finally he raised his head and spoke. "What I want to speak to you about today is the Book of Life. What is it? What must you do to have your name written in it?"

I breathed a sigh of relief. For a moment it appeared that he was going to preach one of those fire-and-brimstone sermons that would make even the staunchest Christian tremble. I had had enough of those during my childhood. Instead, Romero preached a positive message about God's forgiveness, love and grace.

Lucky and I glanced at each other several times. It was obvious that she was uplifted by the sermon. My being laid off from work had been an emotional strain on her. She needed this encouragement and reassurance.

"And now, as we close the service, I wonder if Pastor Nash would come . . .?"

The evangelist paused as our pastor rose from his seat to the right of the platform and walked up the steps to the pulpit. Romero surveyed the congregation, his arms spread wide, inviting all who would come to kneel at the altar and accept Christ as Savior. Two persons stood and made their way to the front as the evangelist continued.

"Anyone who needs a miracle in their life—especially healing of the body, maybe an emotional healing, something to do with financial matters, relationships, anything you would like to have prayer for—please come . . . ."

He spoke softly then, walking from around the back of the podium and down to the steps, he began to pray with the few who had gathered. Lucky turned to me and asked, "Larry, do you think I should get Wess and have him prayed for?"

"What?" I asked incredulously.

Her question surprised and almost annoyed me. Praying for a healing of his diabetes was nothing new to Wesley, us, or the church. We had brought him forward countless times at services just like this, all with the same result—nothing. Wess had become disappointed and discouraged, lately refusing opportunities for prayer. Why should this time be any different?

"You heard what I said," Lucky whispered impatiently.

"Well, honey, if you feel Wess should be prayed for, go get him. I don't really feel one way or another about it."

Excusing herself as she crossed in front of me to the aisle, Lucky hurried to the back of the church. I glanced over my shoulder as she pushed open the doors leading into the small lobby and noticed that Wesley and several other children were waiting for the service to end.

Children's church must have let out early, or the service is running late, I mused. A glance at my watch told me the meeting was running overtime. Lucky was kneeling on one knee facing Wesley and holding him by his hands. He was smiling and nodding his head, both of them framed by the open doors. Lucky stood and led him by the hand across the back of the auditorium and up the side aisle to where I was standing.

Lucky's bouyancy lifted my spirits, too. We walked

up to the stage and waited for our turn to come before the evangelist. . . .

After Romero prayed for Wesley, we told him how his sermon had encouraged us. He thanked us, ruffling Wesley's hair. By this time, most of the people had left the sanctuary and were talking and laughing in the parking lot. Wesley ran ahead.

"Do you think he's healed, Larry?" Lucky looked up at me, her eyes pleading for reassurance.

"I don't . . . know."

I needed to ponder this. How many times had we prayed for our son—fifty, a hundred? Lucky squinted and lowered her head as we walked into the bright sunshine.

"Oh, I *hope* so. I feel so positive about it this time."

Lucky saw Wesley across the parking lot by our car and looked up at me again. "He wants to be healed so much, Larry. He wants so much to be . . . like the other kids."

"I know, honey. I know."

"Praise the Lord, Wesley's healed!" a friend called.

"Yeah, isn't that wonderful? Wesley's . . . healed." Lucky glanced at me nervously.

As I unlocked and opened the car, I realized again my mistake in leaving the windows rolled up. The inside was as hot as a blast furnace. Lucky went to the nursery to get our other son, Jay, while I let it cool down.

Wesley's willingness to be prayed for again surprised me. I had been discouraged and disappointed, maybe even a little bitter, because God had not healed my son before. How deep the grooves of doubt had been cut into my mind as many other times we had prayed futilely for his healing. Yet just a week ago I had testified during a Bible study how the Lord was building my faith. At that time someone had felt impressed that the group should gather around me and pray.

No, I would not doubt this time. I would make a stand and believe.

Our youngest daughter, Patsy, derailed my train of thought as she slammed the car door and yelled, "Come on, Dad, let's go home—I'm hungry!"

Lucky had just arrived with Jay in her arms, and we piled into the car. The seats were still hot, and my shirt was beginning to stick to my back as I started the engine.

"Next car we get, we're going to have air conditioning. I'll never again make the mistake of buying a car in cool weather. Boy, it's hot!" I grumbled.

As we drove home along Mountain View, the warm wind blowing through the open windows cooled me down somewhat and cleared my head. I turned down our street firmly convinced: *I will believe.*

"I got healed today!"

Wesley was standing in the middle of a circle with his neighborhood friends, excitedly telling them what had happened that morning. The other children had just stepped from our church's Sunday school bus, which usually stopped in front of our house. We had changed clothes, and Lucky was getting ready to start dinner.

Pam had darted out the door and was starting to tell the children about the miracle, and Wess had followed close on her heels. "Don't you tell 'em. I want to!"

We peeked through the curtains to see what their big rush was all about.

"I got healed today!" he was crowing.

"Really? Is that true?"

"Whataya mean?"

"Are you sure?"

"How do you know?"

"The Lord really healed you today?"

The children seemed puzzled and surprised.

"Yes, I'm healed!"

"Can you eat whatcha want now?"

"Yeah, guess so!"

Staring out the window, Lucky said blankly, "Oh, look! Wesley's telling his friends that he's healed."

"Yeah," I answered, then thought, *but what if he's not?* I shook my head slightly to rid my mind of that doubt, then looked at Lucky and smiled.

"Yeah. He's healed. . . ."

Lucky grabbed me around the waist tightly as we continued to watch the scene in front of our house. With the yellow school bus as a backdrop, Wess turned to each of his friends as he talked, the early afternoon sun glinting off his shiny brown hair, his hands moving animately to his conversation.

He seems to be positive, I mused. *Perhaps the Lord is going to come through this time.* Lucky turned from the window and walked into the kitchen to continue preparing the meal.

"He seems so convinced that he's well," she laughed. "I believe he *is*." She peered around the corner at me with outward joyful conviction.

"I think you're right," I nodded. That small nagging doubt had returned, however. *But what if we're not right? What if he's not cured? What will that do to his faith?* I couldn't voice these fears to Lucky. *Be positive; speak words of encouragement . . . faith.*

After our meal, we went into the living room and began reading our Bibles while the children played. Jay had fallen into a restless sleep in his crib.

"Let's read through Psalm seventy-eight together," she suggested after several moments of silence. "I'm reading through it now, and it's really causing me to turn my thoughts toward believing God and not doubting Him. . . ."

I stiffened. *Did she know me so well that she could sense doubts? Could she read my mind?* Suddenly I realized that she wanted to be positive and full of faith but was struggling with the same fears. I turned in my Bible to where Lucky was reading.

> That they might *set their hope in God*, and *not forget the works of God*, but keep his commandments:
> And might not be as their fathers, a stubborn and rebellious generation; a generation that set not their heart aright, and whose spirit was not *steadfast with God*.
> The children of Ephraim, being armed, and carrying bows, *turning back in the day of battle*.

As Lucky finished, I pondered God's promises, remembering especially three Bible passages that had been taught to me all my life:

> Whatsoever ye shall bind on earth shall be bound in heaven: and whatsoever ye shall loose on earth shall be loosed in heaven. Again I say unto you, That if two of you shall agree on earth as touching any thing that they shall ask, it shall be done for them of my Father which is in heaven.
>
> Matthew 18:18, 19

> Whosoever shall say unto this mountain, Be thou removed, and be thou cast into the sea; and shall not doubt in his heart, but shall believe that those

things which he saith shall come to pass; he shall have whatsoever he saith. Therefore I say unto you, What things soever ye desire, when ye pray, believe that ye receive them, and ye shall have them.

Mark 11:23, 24

If ye abide in me, and my words abide in you, ye shall ask what ye will, and it shall be done unto you.

John 15:7

Reading these verses, I couldn't help ask myself, *Aren't we Christians, living for the Lord, in His perfect will? Yes. Then why shouldn't these words of Jesus be applied to us? No reason why not. . . .*

Sitting in the quiet summer heat of our living room, Lucky and I resolved to fight doubt all the way.

That night we went to church early. I went to choir practice, the children played with friends on the church day school playground as Lucky watched.

After choir practice, Pastor Nash and several men from the choir gathered in one of the school rooms and shared what had been on our hearts through the week. When the others had left, I buttonholed Pastor Nash.

"Brother Nash, I want to talk to you about this morning . . . about Wesley's healing."

"Okay, shoot."

He seemed open, sensing my need to talk.

"I really think God healed him this morning."

Pastor Nash's face brightened. "He did? Well, that's fantastic, Larry."

Walking out of the classroom and into the courtyard, we strolled up the walkway toward the sanctuary.

"I really feel God encouraging me. The Lord is increasing my faith. God is . . . completing Wesley's healing," I spoke positively to further strengthen my conviction.

"Hey, that's great. That's something the people would love to hear. I'll mention it in the service tonight. You know how long we've all been praying that this would happen."

By the time we reached the door to the auditorium, I was feeling high as a kite. As I floated into the church on my cloud of faith, the choir was singing. I paraded onto the platform, not embarrassed in the least by my lateness. I took my place and began singing with all my might. . . .

As we prepared for bed that night, my exuberance had subsided, leaving a residue of quiet faith. Meanwhile, Lucky was busy with our fussy toddler. As I laid down to sleep, my mind raced across the events of the day. Slowly strange, frightening thoughts began to creep into my reverie. *What if Wesley shows sugar in his urine tomorrow morning? What should I do? What do I tell him? Lord, forgive me. Wesley's healed. Your Word promises . . . .*

I tossed restlessly in bed. Lucky was up and down during the night with Jay because he was restless. About two in the morning I relieved Lucky while she went to bed. After Jay fell asleep, I decided to pray for Wesley. I felt a strong urge to thank God for his healing instead of asking.

Wide awake, I stayed up until dawn. Wondering. Thinking. *Lord, how do we instruct our children about faith? What do we tell them when we say that*

You heal, when we pray for them, and they're not healed? What will that do to their faith? Should I encourage Wess to hold on to his healing by faith? My mind drifted in this manner for many moments, then riveted to a point in my past when a misunderstanding about faith started me on a path to disappointment.

Two years before, I was enrolled in a Bible college in Santa Cruz, California, several hundred miles from Barstow. Feeling led into the ministry, I took advantage of a lay-off from work to begin preparation. Perfect timing! Or so I thought.

As it turned out, I ended up dropping out of school after six weeks. Our house wouldn't sell, and I was commuting to Santa Cruz every week, coming home only on weekends. Our money ran out (we had hoped to live on our home equity and part-time work), and Lucky had delivered our fourth child, Jay, just two weeks before I started. The pressures of Wesley's illness, our financial problems, and my absence was intensely trying to her. She felt that God was distant, that I had deserted her, and that the church didn't understand. She was too shy to tell anyone how deeply she was hurting. Despite these feelings, Lucky didn't want to hinder me from doing God's will. Yet I painfully faced my circumstances and took the only course open to me.

I shared with my psychology professor my unhappy decision to drop out of school. His response, though meant to be encouraging, did nothing to lift my sagging spirit.

"Sometimes things get worse before they get better," he counseled. How true that statement became!

In disappointment I began to question my relationship with God: If He called me to college, why was I forced to quit? Did God let me down? These questions knawed at my heart, leaving crusts of bitterness toward God and His church. *Why should I serve You, Lord, if You're going to lead me on, then dump me just when the desires of my heart are being fulfilled? What kind of a God are You, anyway?* I grumbled.

Sometimes in church services I felt like throwing the Bible on the floor, stomping out, and yelling to the congregation, "Hey! Who are you kidding? It just doesn't work!" Yet patiently and surely, God drew me back from the brink of disaster. I did not know how fervently others were praying for me at this time. A year later, an elderly woman in our church revealed her prayerful concern.

"I've been praying earnestly for you, Larry," she said lovingly. "A very definite impression came to me. In my mind's eye, I saw you standing on a precipice, a very high cliff, and you were about to step off. You were bitter towards God, and your anger was driving you to spiritual suicide. You felt that the bottom had dropped from under your life."

I was stunned. How could she have known? Surely, the Holy Spirit had spoken, and the prayers of this woman had held me back from that fall . . . .

Sitting in a chair in the boys' room, I reflected on that experience. What had I learned? It had strengthened my faith. It had shown me that no matter what happens, God is never wrong. He's always loving, always going to keep us spiritually and physically safe.

I recalled a sermon about stepping out in faith preached by the president of the Bible college. All my life I had been taught that if you could get enough faith to ignore the external circumstances, your faith would be complete. The president's illustration of moving out into the deep water of faith came back to me now.

". . . You must swim out until there's no ground under you, no support at all, *except* the buoyancy of that deep water of faith," he had said. "Let Christ lift you up . . . float in your faith in God . . . strike out for that deep faith!"

Strike out for deep faith . . . That's what we're doing now. As my racing mind began to slow, the warm summer night pressed itself into my every pore, forcing me to relax. Sleepily my thoughts returned to Wess. *What makes me sure that he's healed? Well, his attitude for one thing. Never has he been more positive! He testified of his healing, didn't he? Somehow this time it's different. Lucky and I even feel stronger about it.*

A sudden thought jolted me from my fitful doze in the chair, and a twinge of panic made me sit up straight with a start. *Should I stop Wesley's insulin injections if he shows signs of sugar in his urine in the morning? Oh, God, please help me . . . what should I do?*

3

No Matter
What Happens

The murmuring of the children's voices through the walls, the shuffling of feet in the hallway, the opening and closing of doors: My household was rising. Back in bed, I had fallen soundly asleep just as the first purplish tones of dawn crept through our bedroom window. Golden sunshine streamed through it now, and I looked at our alarm clock on the night stand by my side of the bed.

Eight o'clock. Yawning, I threw back the covers. Sitting up, feet on the floor, sleep draining slowly from my head, my mind cleared. Hearing the familiar noise of Wesley's bath water running into the tub, I stiffened. It was time for Wess to check his urine for sugar.

The struggle of the previous night returned: *What if Wesley's test shows that he needs insulin? Give him a . . . no . . . I'm going to stand on God's Word. He must honor His Word. If the test is positive, it's a lie from Satan, and I'm not going to believe external signs. I'm going to ask God to remove those symptoms and complete the process of healing.*

I stood up, quickly slipped on a pair of trousers and a tee-shirt, then headed down the hallway. As I entered the living room, Lucky seemed relieved. She too had been struggling over the insulin and was glad that I had awakened in time to make the decision.

"How much sleep did you get? How late did Jay

keep you up?" she asked as I plopped down on the couch next to her.

Ignoring her questions, I exclaimed, "I've made the decision. Wesley's healed, and any symptoms we see are a lie from Satan!"

Our conversation was interrupted by the sound of Wesley opening the bathroom door. Glancing quickly in our direction, he stepped toward the kitchen to prepare his insulin injection. The sad expression on his face told it all—the test was positive. Wesley had resigned himself to an uncertain future chained to the life-giving habit of those painful shots. More than ever I wanted him to be free from that bondage.

As Wesley opened the refrigerator door, I saw in my mind's eye his measured activity: Reaching for the two tiny bottles of insulin, one for instant relief, the other for slow-release throughout the day, he closed the door and set the bottles on the kitchen counter. Opening the cupboard door, he reached in and drew out a plastic-wrapped disposable syringe. Unwrapping it and un-capping the fine, sharp needle—holding first one bottle, then the other, up to the light streaming through the window—he carefully punctured each rubber cap with the needle and drew the precious liquid into the syringe, cautiously measuring the corresponding doses from each one. After recapping the needle, he set the syringe on the counter, picked up the bottles, and turn-ed to open the refrigerator door.

With the clinking catsup, mustard, relish, tabasco and salad dressing bottles in the refrigerator door an-nouncing its opening, I could imagine Wesley putting the small bottles inside. The door closed with a soft thud and a loud tinkle of glass. A few seconds later, Wesley appeared at the entrance to the living room, his right hand carrying the insulin-filled syringe. My heart broke as he reluctantly gestured for me to give him his shot. His small face carried years of disappointment and despair in that one moment . . . .

"Wesley, we're not going to believe that test," I spoke firmly, standing to my feet. "It's just a lie of Satan. You are healed."

I took the syringe from his hand, strode to the wastebasket and squirted the insulin into the trash, broke off the needle so it could not be used again, and threw the syringe into the wastebasket. Wesley's eyes opened wide—he had never seen me move with such deftness and determination. I was even a little surprised myself. A smile crept across his puzzled face, bursting into a grin as I took him by the shoulders.

"We believe you are healed, son," I repeated gently. He threw his arms around me and hugged tightly. Tears began to form in my eyes. "You are healed, Wess," I said again, holding him there, just for that small, wonderful moment—one did not hold on long to a child as active as Wesley. Breaking free, he gazed up at me, grinning in agreement, then bounded into the kitchen to fix his own breakfast. That one look said everything: He was looking to me for encouragement, for the strength to throw away his insulin.

"Hey, Mom!" he called. "Can I have sugar on my cereal this morning?"

Lucky, who had shared our tender moment, darted a nervous glance up at me, "Sure, honey, if you're . . . healed, go ahead."

Noticing the anxiety flashing through her eyes, I understood her feelings of panic—our actions this morning were against all the doctor's orders. And yet, we needed to exercise our faith, didn't we?

I patted her on the shoulder. "It'll be all right, Lucky. It's just a test of faith. You'll see."

As Wesley happily sprinkled the sugar on his milk-drenched corn flakes, we hurried the girls out the front door toward the car for the drive across town to Vacation Bible School. The rest of the day was routine enough, and Wesley came in only occasionally from playing with a neighbor boy to go to the bathroom or ask for a banana. We didn't give his condition much thought until late in the afternoon when Lucky was preparing dinner. She was the first to notice that his trips to the restroom were becoming more frequent. A bad sign: His sugar level was rising.

"Larry. . . ?"

"Yeah, I don't like it, either."

Fear flashed through both of us at the same time.

"There's a service at your brother's church tonight, Larry. Would you mind if I go? I need something more from the Lord to strengthen me," she almost cried.

"No. You go ahead. I'll stay home with the kids," I smiled weakly. . . .

The door slammed shut, and Lucky strode excitedly into the house. Surprised at the suddenness of her entry, I looked up from what I was doing and stared at her blankly. My brother, Tony, and his wife, Carol, followed.

"Hi! Tony, Carol. Come in. Have a seat." I gestured toward the chairs near them. "How was the meeting, honey?"

"Well, you know how I was this evening. . . ."

I nodded, remembering.

". . . Well, I was so worried that Wesley wasn't healed—I mean, he still had the symptoms. So I stood up and testified in the middle of the meeting that he was healed. Really positively confessed my faith and thanked the Lord. After the service, I went up to the altar and prayed. I feel better now. . . ."

As Lucky went on with her story, I gradually felt envious. *Why couldn't I have gotten away for just a little while?* Although it had been a fairly normal day, the added anxiety of watching Wesley was just a bit too much for me. I shrugged, smiled politely, and continued to listen to the evening's details.

". . . and Brother Hall, you know, Tony's pastor—he's such a nice young man—he stood and let . . . ."

Our front door slammed open, and in burst Wesley.

"Oh. . . ." I muttered, glancing at my watch, suddenly remembering that I had told him that he could watch T.V. with our neighbor boy at his home until ten o'clock.

Lucky was justifiably amazed, for Wesley was usually in bed by this time.

"It's ten-o-five, son," I scowled teasingly.

"Sorry, Dad," Wesley stammered.

I rubbed my chin vigorously to disguise the grin slowly inching itself up my face. Seeing me trying to hide my amusement, Wess ran over to the couch and threw his arms around my neck. The impact nearly knocked my glasses off. Lucky, Tony, and Carol burst into laughter at the sight of Wess clinging to his off-balance dad almost falling off the couch with his glasses askew.

"I promise I'll never be late again, Dad, I promise," Wess pretended to whine. He unwrapped his arms from around my neck, got up, turned, and stepped quickly to his mom, then gave her a quick kiss and a hug.

"G'night, Mom, Dad, Uncle Tony, Aunt Carol," he called back from the hall. His bedroom door closed behind him.

Exhausted, I soon excused myself and went to bed. At first sleep came fitfully. Anything—a bump in the attic, the cracking of the outside walls cooling in the still-warm summer night—would jerk me into full wakefulness. Suddenly, the long mournful howl of a lonely dog baying at the full moon rising over the barren eastern ridge of the valley drew me once more out of my stupified sleep and into a painful, yearning consciousness. Again, the dog howled.

Was that Wesley moaning? No . . . guess it was just a dog. Oh, God, please help me sleep. As I lay there in bed, my hopes for more deep unconsciousness slipped away, my prayer unanswered. Gently tossing off the sheet, I moved carefully to not disturb Lucky's sleep and slowly creaked over to the chair where my trousers had been laid. Putting them on, I lost my balance and almost tumbled. Despite the warm night, the continuing howls sent a chill through my body.

Lord, what's happening to me? Why can't I relax? Why am I so full of fear?

I stepped slowly into the hall from our bedroom, carefully navigating by feeling the walls. Cracking open Wesley's door, I peeked in and breathed a silent, grateful sigh. *At least he's sleeping all right.* Then my heart froze.

In the gentle moonlight beaming through the bedroom window, I noticed the large, slightly shiny spot surrounding his groin. *He's wet the bed!*

Wess had wet the bed before, when his diabetes had gotten out of control. This was a sure sign that his body was craving insulin. Again, doubt and confusion filled my mind. Should I continue to claim Wesley's healing when the obvious symptoms showed that he was not? Was this also a lie of Satan, intended to make me deny my son's healing?

Quietly closing Wesley's door, I padded slowly into the living room and slumped onto the couch. With elbows on my knees and hands cradling my head, I tried to pray.

Moments later, I stood and stole quietly past Wesley's bedroom and down the hall toward mine. As I settled in bed, Lucky stirred, moaned, and turned over to face me with a troubled expression on her face. She was not sleeping as soundly as I had thought. It was about four o'clock when I again drifted off to a restless sleep.

Tuesday morning Lucky was feeling encouraged. "Honey, we can't give up. God's going to heal him," she said cheerfully, seeing my obvious distress. "Remember the lady with the goiter?"

I nodded.

"She had it prayed for, and went about confessing that it was gone. Acting on 1 Peter 2:24, '. . . by whose stripes ye *were* healed', she didn't acknowledge the goiter and it soon disappeared.

"Then there's the man who wrote how God told him that the symptoms are not the same as the cause of sickness. He had been healed, yet Satan was causing the symptoms to return to make him deny his healing.

"He says you have to stand on God's promises and claim them. Larry, that means we have to believe God's Word, not what we are seeing. We have to *trust* God to deliver Wesley. Maybe we don't see the answer yet because God wants to test our faith."

"Yeah, that's true," I mumbled. "Maybe we should throw Wesley's insulin away."

"His healing may hinge on whether we act on our faith or not, so I guess we should," Lucky agreed.

She went to the refrigerator, withdrew all of the insulin, and tossed it into the trash can.

Soon Roberta Palmer came by to take Pam and Pat to Vacation Bible School and Lucky to the women's Bible study. Wesley was in bed, but appeared okay when they left. Watching Jay play with Wess on his bed, I strengthened my resolve. I decided to take the trash can to the dump, so we wouldn't give in to temptation later.

"Wess, keep Jay in there with you for a few minutes. I'm going to the dump. Be back in a little while."

Wesley's stomach was aching when I returned. Laying my hand on his abdomen, I knelt by his bed and prayed. "Father, in Jesus' name I ask, take away the pain, and the cause of the pain."

Tossing a ball to Jay, Wesley smiled, "My stomach feels better now, but my head hurts a little."

Feeling encouraged, I called Lucky at the Bible study. ". . . he's getting better, but he has a headache," I reported.

"Well, I'll have the ladies pray for him," Lucky offered.

I had just hung up the phone when a soft groan turned my head toward the bedroom. Stepping quickly through the dining room and into the hall, I stopped in front of the open doorway to Wesley's room. Wearing nothing but cotton brief-style underwear, he was laying on his back with his arms folded across his stomach, and his hands clutching each side of his abdomen.

"Oh, God, why did I take that insulin to the dump?" I muttered to myself in anger. "How could I have thrown that stuff away?"

Helplessly, I watched my son hobble out of bed and into the bathroom where he threw up. I checked on him constantly after that. The sight of him lying in bed, pale, clutching his stomach, lolling his head about on the pillow, moaning at times, sent my panic soaring. He looked over at me standing in the doorway and spoke weakly: "Dad, my stomach hurts again, and my head aches. I hurt all over. Please pray for me."

As I knelt at his bedside, I laid my hands on Wesley's stomach. "Please, Jesus—take away these symptoms," I begged. "Manifest your healing in Wesley now. Please, God. . . ." My voice cracked in falsetto as I buried my face in his bed. Was it wrong to weaken now? Was God allowing our son's symptoms to linger and grow worse just to test our faith? Should we withhold his insulin . . .no matter what happens?

I stepped briskly to the phone and dialed. "Lucky, I've got to get some insulin. Wesley's worse! We should never have thrown it away this morning. I can't stand seeing him suffer like this anymore. Come home so I can go to the drug store."

If Lucky had not understood my words over the telephone, she certainly could not have mistaken the panic in my voice.

"Wait, Larry. Wait right there. We've been praying over here, and we have the victory about Wesley's healing," she reassured.

"Lucky, you don't understand! I just can't stand it anymore. Wesley's *not* getting better. He's in pain. Suffering. I want to give him some insulin," I sobbed.

"We're almost finished praying . . . wait a minute. I'll ask some of the ladies if they'll come home with me to pray. . . . We'll be right over."

Lucky hung up, and I remained in the dining room

for a moment, holding the phone to my ear while the dial tone began to hum. Slowly, I placed the receiver into its cradle, my mind blank with exhaustion. I had had very little food or sleep for the past two days, constantly struggling and striving for God to complete the healing of my son.

Trodding into the living room, I reached for my Bible on the lamp stand, flipped it open, and scanned the page looking for comfort. I read a sentence somewhere in the middle of a chapter, and immediately pushed it to the back of my mind.

God's not saying that. I only read it because it was underlined, I reasoned.

No. God's not saying that . . . .

4

"Father . . . This Innocent Child of Yours"

Kneeling at Wesley's bedside a few minutes later, I heard our front door open, heralding shuffling feet and concerned whispers. Lucky appeared at Wesley's door, then several of the women from the Bible study peeked in.

"We came right over, Larry," Joyce Bannister spoke encouragingly. She was a large pretty woman whose size was matched by the bigness of her heart. "We want to stand with you and Lucky in this."

As Lucky knelt next to me, the other women filed quietly into the room. Joyce, Cindy Wilson, Beth Johnson, Karen Wilson, Roberta Palmer—one by one, they took their places behind us, some laying hands on our shoulders, others simply standing, eyes closed, intent on prayer.

"Lord, we pray for strength . . . . Heal Wess, dear Jesus; let the manifestation of your healing appear even now. We command these symptoms to go and Satan to loose his hold on this boy, in Jesus' name. Jesus, let your healing mercies flow upon Wesley. . . ."

As prayers filled the room, we felt uplifted, encouraged, and convinced to hold on for his healing.

The atmosphere warmed, melting the chill that had tightly gripped my heart that morning.

We didn't realize how loudly we were praying until Wess blurted irritably, "My head hurts; could you be quiet?" A stunned hush fell on us. I looked at Lucky—some of the women's eyes were wide with surprise.

"Okay, Wess. We're sorry."

He moaned and turned away from us as Lucky led everyone to the living room. She returned as we sat in silence for a long while. Joyce, Cindy, and Karen sat opposite me on the couch, eyes closed, lips moving in silent prayer. On the piano bench, Roberta gazed pensively at the floor. Joyce bowed forward slightly to fervently but gently and quietly pound her fists into her knees. I glanced at Beth, sitting to my left in a wooden rocker, who avoided my gaze to nervously watch the others on the couch. She then glared at me.

"What's going on, Larry?" she demanded.

I heaved a sigh, and explained, "Wesley was prayed for last Sunday, Beth, and we're just waiting for that healing to. . . ."

"But why is he suffering so much?"

"Beth," I answered gently—this was new to her, and I wanted to explain our situation as simply as possible—. . . we feel that Wesley is going to be well, but that God is testing our faith now to see how serious we are about getting Wess' healing. God wants us to believe His Word and promises strong enough to ignore these symptoms. He wants us to hang on. Wesley *is* healed—we just have to wait on the Lord for Him to take away the symptoms."

Looking in on Wesley a few minutes later, I was again confronted with the reality of his suffering. My heart sank once more.

"Larry, you haven't been out of the house since Sunday. Why don't you go out . . . do something . . . go for a walk," Lucky pleaded when she noticed my depression. I stood in the middle of the room for a moment, thinking. *Karl Kessler—I'll go see Karl. I glanced at my watch. Almost four. He'll be getting off work pretty soon. I'll drive down to the Marine base where he works and meet him at the gate. . . .*

I stood next to my car in the motel parking lot near the gate. Karl was a good friend and a strong Christian who knew his Bible. For several minutes the sun beat the fatigue and cold disappointment out of my exhausted body while I watched the cars driving out of the base. No Karl.

Disappointed, I got into my car, eased into the sparce traffic trickling out of the base, and headed along the highway toward Karl's home.

"Hey, Larry, how's it goin', brother? Good to see you!" Karl's big voice greeted me as he opened the door to my knock. "Come on in!"

I stepped into his home, noticing how cool it was inside, and remembering that he had recently installed a new water cooler. "Swamp coolers" we call them out in the desert.

My anguish began to pour as though someone had broken a dam. ". . . you know, he's really suffering," I almost wept. "It's so hard to watch your son suffer like that, especially when you know that if you give him insulin he's going to stop suffering. Yet if I do that, Karl, I'd be going against what God wants. I'd be denying the faith for his healing, and then he'd lose it because I'm weak." My words sounded hollow. My confidence in God was shaken.

Karl understood my feelings. Once his son had been seriously ill, and he had depended solely on prayer for the boy's recovery.

"Why don't you come over and pray with us, Karl," I continued. A thin ray of hope shined through at the thought of Karl joining our vigil. He agreed, and I began to feel relieved.

When we arrived, the women had left to attend their families. Dinner time came and went as Karl, Lucky, and I continued to pray. Tony and Carol dropped by on their way to church. Learning that Wesley was so ill, Tony stayed with us. Carol took Pam, Pat and Jay with her to the service. When they returned, Pastor Hall was with them. Caught up in our cause, he was convinced that Wesley would be healed. "Hang on," he would say. "Jesus will heal."

Many of our friends periodically came and went throughout the day, returning to pray and to see Wesley's progress until midnight. Meanwhile, he had been getting worse, vomiting and urinating continually, drinking much water to quench his flaming thirst. The other children and I went to bed long before the last visitor left, leaving Lucky alone at Wesley's bedside.

I couldn't sleep. In my mind's eye I kept seeing my son, slipping in and out of consciousness. In the other room by the dim light of a small lamp, Lucky was reading verses from the Bible on healing.

Bless the Lord, O my soul, and forget not all his benefits: who forgiveth all thine iniquities; who healeth all thy diseases. . . .

He was wounded for our transgressions, he was bruised for our iniquities: the chastisement of our peace was upon him; and *with his stripes we are healed.*

> Psalm 103:2, Isaiah 53:5

About two in the morning, Wesley mumbled what sounded to Lucky like, "Jay's outside, go get him." Bending over Wess, she whispered, "No, he isn't. Jay's in the other room asleep."

"No!" Wesley insisted. "He's outside. Go get him. See? He's outside."

"No, Wesley, he's not outside; he's okay. . . ."

Lucky believed Satan was reacting to the Bible verses she was quoting and was attempting through Wess to get her out of the room; the devil didn't want her to pray and read God's Word. Seeing these as hours of warfare with the devil, she determined to fight even more when Wesley complained about the light.

"Roll over and face the wall so it won't bother you," she urged, draping a towel over the shade to deflect the shine. *I'm not going to turn the lamp off, Devil,* Lucky asserted. *You just want me to quit praying. I'm not giving up!*

I squinted at the alarm clock on the nightstand. *Three-thirty.* Frustrated and wide awake, I joined Lucky, burying my face in our son's bed, letting out my anguish in fervent prayer. By now Wesley's breathing had become more labored.

"God! Heal my son . . . in Jesus' name!" I demanded loudly.

"Shh," Lucky hissed sharply. "You'll wake up the other kids."

My thoughts were deeply troubled. *Why hasn't Wesley been healed yet? We have prayed for so long, yet the symptoms persist. Maybe he's not well because*

I haven't contacted my spiritual leader. Surely God won't let Wess die. He won't permit all this suffering forever. Maybe when Pastor Nash arrives, the healing will be manifested.

I jumped up and practically ran into the dining room to the telephone. Hand on the receiver, I glanced at my watch. *Four o'clock. Maybe I ought to wait until about seven.* Wesley's labored breathing wafted through the hallway to where I stood. *He's our pastor, and we need him now!*

I dialed quickly. The phone's receiver buzzed once, twice, three, four times in my ear before a sleepy baritone voice answered.

"Y-yes, uh, this is the Nash residence . . . can I help you?"

"Pastor, this is Larry . . . Larry Parker. We need you right away! Wesley's very sick."

"Okay, Larry. I'll be right over."

The phone clicked, and I quickly hung up and walked back into Wesley's room. About fifteen minutes later, a loud rap on the front door interrupted our silent vigil. Drawing the pastor inside quickly, I led him into the bedroom. He sat in a chair at Wesley's feet, and I sat at his head, all three of us praying quietly for several minutes. Pastor Nash then laid hands on Wesley's clammy body and began to pray aloud.

"Father, we bring before You this innocent child of Yours, who needs a special touch from Your healing hand . . . ."

I closed my eyes and allowed his soothing voice to carry me in its firm concern. Wesley's chest continued to rise sporatically, gasping, quietly choking for air. He was still unconscious even after the prayer. I looked at my spiritual leader in dismay, having fully expected

Wess to be lying there peaceful, resting after his long physical trial. Totally healed.

Suddenly, Wesley's eyes fluttered open, and he turned his head to look at me. "I'm thirsty. Need to go to the bathroom," he whispered hoarsely through chapped lips, reaching out to me with his left arm.

Lucky knew that Wess was shy. "I'll leave the room," she offered.

Pastor Nash stood and whispered, "I'll go into the other room to pray, Larry. Be back in a little while."

They walked slowly, quietly out of the room. I lifted Wess up on the bed so he could go into a small pot I had brought in for that purpose. He seemed so limp and fragile on my arm.

He didn't urinate, so I gave Wesley a small plastic cup half-filled with water. As he weakly sipped through a wax-paper straw, gulping and slurping the water down his parched throat, my mind wandered: He had gotten the cup from McDonalds. For some reason, Wess loved that cup. Maybe it was the clown painted on the side. I recalled the day he brought it home and proudly showed it to his mom.

Wess spat out the straw and gasped, "Enough. I don't . . . want any . . . more."

He began to breathe again with much difficulty as I laid him back down.

At intervals throughout the three-hour vigil with Pastor Nash, Lucky would leave the room unable to bear her son's suffering. Now as I tried to get Wess to use his pot and drink from the McDonalds cup, Lucky was in the living room doing battle with the Lord. At the first glimmer of dawn the bitterness she had begun to harbor toward God over Wesley's agony reached its peak. *God! Why don't you do something? Why are you*

*allowing his suffering to continue? Haven't we proven
our faith to You yet?*

Kneeling beside the couch, she clenched her fists and
pounded the floor. "If You let Wesley die, I'm going to
turn my back on You; I won't serve You any longer!"
she sobbed. "Please, God. Let me see my son's healing.
Oh, Jesus, please. Don't let him suffer so . . . any
longer."

She remembered the story in the Bible when many
of Jesus' followers had forsaken Him over one of His
teachings. Jesus asked His closest disciples if they were
going to leave, too. Peter was the first to express their
faithfulness, "Where can we go? No one else has the
words of eternal life." Reflecting upon those words,
Lucky was afraid to make good her threat. Jesus was
her ticket to Heaven. Without Him, she'd go to Hell.

"Okay, Lord, if You don't do something to help
Wesley by the time the stores open, I'm going to buy
some insulin. I can't stand this any more!"

Embarrassed when Pastor Nash caught her in those
moments of anguish, Lucky quickly stood and walked
sheepishly to the end of the hallway. It was then that
Wesley spoke some strange words, which made us
believe that a sinister force was hindering his recovery.

Unwittingly we were about to enter a twilight zone
of deception.

"We won't let you have the gifts," Wess announced
loud enough for Lucky to hear clearly.

Shocked because he wasn't in a state to speak so
coherently, I bent low. "What did you say?"

"We won't let you have the gifts," Wesley repeated
firmly.

Nothing about his voice was different, but his attitude had suddenly changed. It was unlike our son. I

was convinced that he had not spoken on his own, that Wesley was under satanic influence. In the hallway, Lucky had the same impression.

Wesley was never possessed by an evil spirit, for he loved Jesus and was a child of God. But because of what had just happened, we believed a demon was responsible for his illness—certainly for his seeming lack of recovery, even in the presence of so much prayer, Bible reading and faith. With this in mind, I determined to rid Wesley of the devil.[1]

"In the name of Jesus, you leave," I spoke sharply to the invisible entity.

The presence fled, and immediately Wesley's breathing became easier. Soon he was able to sit up and urinate into the pot.

Lucky and Pastor Nash entered the room. "Wesley's better! He's breathing okay," I cried jubilantly. "We've had a victory! A demon was in his pancreas and was feeding on his insulin. But its gone! Wesley's pancreas will begin to produce insulin now, and in a matter of hours he'll be back to his old self again!"

The signs of weariness in Lucky's face faded, and she brightened with joy.

"He's healed! Praise God, he's healed! The battle's over, and we've won the victory!" We rejoiced as relief swept us like a healing balm.

Pastor Nash observed the scene with caution. "Guess you don't need me now," he smiled quietly. "It's seven o'clock. Think I'll go over to the church and pray."

---

1. We had little understanding of demonology and deliverance and were reacting instinctively at this point.

"Everything's going to be okay now, Pastor," I responded. "Thanks for coming over and standing with us. We really appreciate that."

He waved to us in the bright early sunshine of that Wednesday morning before getting into his car across the street. The air was cool and refreshing. Joyfully, we waved back as he slipped into his seat, started the engine, and slowly drove up the hill toward the church.

With new hope, we relaxed on the living room couch, leaving Wesley by himself to rest. The temptation to buy more insulin had fled also. We had reached a point of no return. We could never give Wess another shot of insulin, for this would invite that demon to return. But our respite was short lived.

A loud groan from the bedroom stunned us where we sat. Shooting frightened glances at each other, we jumped to our feet and ran to Wesley's room. He was slowly thrashing in pain, and again had begun his rapid, labored breathing.

Lucky looked to me, fear flashing in her eyes. "Oh, Larry, you only cast one demon out. It said 'we,' remember? There must be more."

Turning toward Wesley I exclaimed, "In the name of Jesus, I command you, demon, to leave." This time there was no reaction. Sagging once more under the weight of our heavy burden, we returned to prayer. We sought the protection of the blood of Jesus, not knowing what else to do.

As the morning rose into another blazing summer day, Wesley's condition became steadily worse. Karen and her husband, Eugene, came with Cindy to join us in prayer. We explained what had happened during the early morning hours. Joining hands in a circle around Wesley's bed, we all attempted to cast the demon out. Seeing no response to our commands, we sat down in chairs and prayed silently.

"Larry," a voice broke through my anguish. It was Eugene. "Brother Nash is in the living room. He wants to talk to you."

Emerging from the hall, I noticed that Mark Benkowski, a friend of mine, was with him.

"Do you believe what you're doing is right?" my pastor began.

"Yes. Wesley's been healed, but the devil is causing the symptoms to rob us of that healing."

"Don't you think you should take Wesley to the doctor to confirm his healing?" Pastor Nash countered.

"We will later," I smiled patiently. "Taking him now would only demonstrate doubt."

"Well, I think you're wrong, Larry. I really think you're wrong! You should take Wess to the hospital . . . now. Don't you agree, Mark?"

"Larry, Pastor is right. You should take him to the doctor," Mark frowned with deep concern.

"Well, I appreciate your anxiety—both of you—but I'm Wesley's father, and God has given *me* the faith. I must act on it."

With a look of disappointment, they turned and left. Meanwhile, Lucky had been resting in our bedroom. Eugene had gone to pick up Joyce and had returned. Lucky joined all of us in Wesley's room where we continued our vigil.

I sat on a chair at the head of the bed, clasping Wesley's right hand gently in mine. "Oh, God, *Your* Son suffered for only three hours. Wess has suffered for

days. Oh . . . God, why do You delay . . . why . . . do
You . . . delay?"

Recalling a verse in the Bible where Jesus delayed
His coming to Lazarus until after he died, Lucky
couldn't bear the prospect that this could be happening
to us, and left the room. Joyce followed.

In the living room Joyce put her arms around Lucky
in a comforting hug.

"When I heard Larry pray, 'Oh, God, why do You
delay,' it made me think how Jesus deliberately delayed coming to heal Lazarus because He wanted to
raise him from the dead," Lucky said, weeping.
"Could it be that God wants us to be *willing* to let
Wesley die so that he can be resurrected?"

Joyce's face registered surprise.

"Now don't get me wrong! I don't think God's going
to do that. It's like . . . Abraham and Isaac. God just
wanted Abraham to be *willing* to give up Isaac. He
didn't take him."

Walking into the living room, I overheard Lucky's
conversation. A Bible verse emerged from the back of
my mind where I had pushed it the day before.

"You could be right," I injected. "Yesterday my eyes
fell on Acts 4:10 where the words were underlined
'whom God raised from the dead!' Maybe that *is* what
God wants. Maybe He wants to see if we're willing to
go all the way with Him. Then we'll see Wesley's healing complete."

Soon Eugene and Karen had to go home to their
children. Karen asked if they could take Pam, Pat, and
Jay with them for a visit. My mind reeled at their suggestion. Where had the girls and Jay been all this time?
I hardly remembered them being around.

The girls had gone to Vacation Bible School the last

two mornings, but what about the afternoons and evenings? I searched my dusky memory over the last twenty-four hours and could only recall their worried glances through Wesley's bedroom window, along with the neighborhood children who were curious about what was going on in the Parker home.

The neighbors! What did they think? All the loud praying—it had not occurred to me that we had drawn such attention, even when I saw the large group of children gathered with my own around the outside of the bedroom window.

We agreed to let them go home with Eugene and Karen. We didn't want the children to see Wesley's suffering anymore, not knowing how much longer it would be before his symptoms would vanish. As they were leaving, Lucky shook her head slowly. "It's hard to let them go. Somehow I feel like . . . I won't see them for a long time."

After they had gone, Lucky and I went to our room and laid across the bed, hoping to get some rest. Joyce and Cindy went to Wesley's room. Joyce prayed, "Oh, God, if there is anybody that You want to be here, please send them." Moments later the phone rang, and Lucky answered. It was Sharon Singleton.

"Lucky, I have a burden for Wess. Could I come over and pray?"

"Yes, Sharon. I'm lying down, so would you just come on in when you get here?"

Lucky and I couldn't sleep. Fully clothed, we lay on our stomachs, resting heads on our folded arms. At first we hummed, then began to speak the words of a song, sometimes stopping to weep:

Tis so sweet to trust in Jesus,
just to take Him at His Word;

Just to rest upon His promise;
Just to know, "Thus saith the Lord."

Jesus, Jesus, how I trust Him,
How I've proved Him o'er and o'er.
Jesus, Jesus, precious Jesus!
O for grace to trust Him more.

Unable to stay away from Wess any longer, we continued our vigil in his room. At the head of his bed, I clasped Wesley's right hand in the two of mine. Lucky sat at the foot, and tenderly touched his leg. Sharon, Joyce, and Cindy were seated across from us.

Suddenly, Lucky caught her breath. Wesley's foot looked gray. Cautiously, she touched it. Cold. The realization that death was creeping up his body began to dawn on us. At the same time a strong sense of peace enveloped us. The more we became aware that Wesley was dying, the thicker the atmosphere of peace became. It was a peace that passes all understanding.[2]

We didn't acknowledge the finality of Wesley's passing, for we believed he would soon be resurrected. Perhaps our sense of peace stemmed from this expectation. Yet, the presence of God brings with it a comforting atmosphere that undergirds one in times of crisis.

Lucky began reading from the Twenty-Third Psalm. ". . . yea, though I walk through the valley of the shadow of death, I will fear no evil: for thou art

---

2. Philippians 4:7

with me . . . Thou preparest a table before me in the presence of mine enemies. . . ."

"Wesley's with Jesus now, but he'll be coming back," I said calmly, observing the rising panic in Joyce, Sharon and Cindy. . . .

5

"He Will Rise"

Reliving the nightmare of Wesley's death is no easy task for Lucky and me—even now. But as the second day of our Court trial progressed, the painful process of justice was taking its toll on those who had stood by our side. Among them, Cindy Wilson.

Prosecutor Tom Frazier was relentless in his questioning. I breathed a prayer for her as he began. Here she was, a new Christian, in a court of law intent on holding not only our beliefs up to the scrutiny of the world, but hers also.

"Mrs. Wilson, up to the time that Wesley died, were you able to see that he was breathing and that there was some sign of life?"

"Yes," she answered nervously.

"Did you notice a point where he stopped breathing?"

"When he lifted his leg."

"What happened at that point? What did everyone do?"

"Joyce got scared and jumped up and yelled, 'Larry, something is wrong; we better do something.' Sharon started to cry, and Lucky read the Twenty-third Psalm. Larry was saying he was with Jesus, and I just sat there," Cindy's voice trembled.

After a brief silence, the prosecutor continued his questioning. "At any time while you were at the Parker residence, either on Tuesday or Wednesday, did you observe the Parkers provide any medication to Wesley?"

"No."

Frazier smiled sweetly at Cindy. He was masterfully building the charge of felony child abuse into a convincing case. According to the testimony, it would have appeared that we were unreasonably and heartlessly withholding our son's insulin. Although admiring the prosecutor's cleverness, I shuddered to think that his skill was being used to destroy Lucky and me.

The prosecutor turned his head toward us, raised his smile into a sneer, and turned to Cindy again.

"Now, Mrs. Wilson, other than an occasional drink of water and some prayer, was there anything else that was given to Wesley while you were there?"

Quiet filled the courtroom as Cindy pensively looked down and thought. After a few seconds, she looked straight into Frazier's face and responded:

"Love."

The prosecutor's eyebrows snapped up in surprise. A murmur arose in the gallery.

"By whom?" Frazier demanded quickly.

"His parents."

A thunderbolt of joy thudded into my heart. *Cindy, I love you! Thank you, Jesus.* With one word, she had destroyed hours of testimony for the prosecution.

Frazier stepped back, stiffened, then stepped toward the witness stand. "How did they give him love?" he snapped.

"I don't really know how to tell you, but it was written all over them. I saw their anguish, and they were very gentle with him."

The prosecutor shook his head slightly, and took a

deep breath. "Did you see signs of suffering by Wesley?"

"The heavy breathing."

Frazier paused, then looked up to the judge.

"May I have a moment, Your Honor?"

"Yes," intoned the judge.

The prosecutor stood, thinking, as though he were trying to figure out how to rebuild his case. Finally, he shrugged and fastened his eyes on the judge again.

"I have nothing further."

Judge Williams nodded to Lee Simmons, Lucky's attorney at the Counselors' table. "You may cross examine."

Scooting back the wooden chair in which he was sitting, Lucky's attorney walked quickly around the table and strode toward the stand. He and the prosecutor passed each other, Frazier blankly looking toward the Counselors' table, lost in thought.

The buzzing gallery quieted as Lee began to cross examine Cindy. His voice was kindly, touching the ears gingerly with a hint of compassion and calm.

"Mrs. Wilson, have you composed yourself now; are you less nervous?"

Cindy's eyes darted around the courtroom.

"N-no. . . ."

As the questioning continued, my thoughts returned to the events that had followed Wesley's death. . . .

A few sharp raps at the front door brought me out of Wesley's room and to the front door. Through the window curtains, I could see Tony nervously shifting his weight from one leg to the other.

"Larry, you should take Wesley to the doctor!" he

spoke rapidly as he hurried into the house and stopped one step in front of me. I stood facing him, my arm still holding the door open.

"Well, Tony, that won't be necessary," My voice was calm, strong.

"I know you don't think it's necessary, but if you *don't* take him to a doctor, I'm going to call the police," his voice was rising, crackling with energy, his face beginning to redden.

"Tony, that *won't* be necessary. Wesley's with Jesus now."

"Whataya mean he's 'with Jesus now?' " Tony snapped.

"He's already dead."

Tony's mouth dropped. "Are you sure?"

"Yes, we're sure, but please don't call the police. We believe the Lord's going to raise him up, and we want to pray about that."

"I want to see for myself," Tony muttered in disbelief. Pushing past me, he strode through the living room and made a sharp right turn into the hall. I followed slowly behind. Entering the bedroom, I glanced at the bewildered faces of the women who shared our vigil and shrugged. Tony bent over Wesley with his ear to the chest, then straightened and stared down at the small, still body before him. He slowly turned, staring into space, and murmured, "No heartbeat; he *is* . . . dead."

Tony's blank expression turned to a fascinating mixture of horror and panic. "Do you know what you've done?" he growled.

"Yes," I replied calmly. "Yes, we know. And I have never felt so much peace in my life. We really believe God is about to raise him up."

Tony exhaled slowly, like a balloon having its air let out. "Well, I wish you luck," he spat, walking dejectedly out of the room. "I won't talk to the police. I just want to be by myself and pray." Seconds later the front door opened softly and closed with a click. . . .

The women—Cindy Wilson, Joyce Bannister, and Sharon Singleton followed us aimlessly into the living room where we prayed some more and discussed our next move. A tremendous event was about to happen. I could see the headlines—"Barstow Boy Raised From the Dead!"

An idea began to form in my mind. *Maybe we should take Wesley to the church and have him prayed for. What a setting for his resurrection—up near the altar, where he had been prayed for so many times for healing. Perfect!*

"I'm calling Pastor Nash," I announced, heading for the phone and quickly dialing the church's number.

"Calvary Christian Center. May I help you?" The voice on the other end sounded pleasant, helpful.

"Yes, uh, could I talk with Pastor Nash, please?"

"Yes, may I tell him who's calling?"

"Larry Parker."

The phone clicked on hold, then a baritone voice reverberated cheerfully through the phone receiver.

"Hello, Larry. How's Wesley?"

"He's dead, Pastor, but we believe that God's going to raise him up."

Silence.

"Pastor? Are you there?"

"Y-yes, Larry. I just didn't expect this," he faltered. "I thought for sure that you would have taken him to the hospital."

His voice strengthened like a steam engine building up power.

"No, we believe that the Lord is going to raise. . . ."

"Larry, you should have talked with me about this. I told you to take that boy to the doctor!" Pastor Nash wasn't shouting, but his tone was distinctly angry.

"Well, anyway, this is what we believe will happen. Can we bring Wesley over to have him raised there? We can all get together to pray, and. . . ."

"No, Larry." Pastor Nash's voice was quiet, more controlled. "No, I don't think that would be wise. We'll just pray over here."

"Well, could you pray that God will raise him from the dead?"

Silence again.

"No," he refused finally. "I don't think we should pray for that."

"All right." In dismay I slowly hung up the phone and wandered into the living room. "Imagine that! He wouldn't even pray that Wess would be raised," I complained to the others. . . .

I glanced around the room—Lucky sat on the couch with a look of calmness on her face that I hadn't seen for days. She had been reading out of the Psalms, a great source of encouragement to her. Joyce sat next to Lucky, her head buried in her hands. Sharon sat crying quietly, occasionally wiping away the tears with a Kleenex. In the overstuffed chair to my right, Cindy stared straight ahead into space, sniffing, tear stains lining her face.

A knock on the door fused my attention on the two shadowy shapes visible through the door's window curtains. Wesley had been dead for about an hour. Who could be calling on us at this time? My heart was gripped with fear at the sight of the uniformed policemen idly standing, quietly talking, their backs practically turned to the door.

At the sound of the opening door, the officers quickly turned and smiled. I opened it only part way.

"Yes, may I help you?" I wanted to sound calm, but the words came out gruff and uneven.

"Mr. Parker? Mr. Lawrence Parker?" I glanced down to the questioning patrolman's name tag: Joe Pedroza.

"Uh, I—yes, I'm Larry Parker. Whataya want?"

"Well, Mr. Parker, we have a complaint here." The officer glanced down at his small tablet of paper. "There's been a death in your home?"

"Yes, my son just died . . . about an hour ago."

"Well, sir, would you let us in?" Pedroza's voice was smooth, polite, professional.

"Do you have a warrant?" I snapped.

"No, I don't have a warrant. . . ." He tossed a questioning glance at his fellow officer. ". . . but we would like to come in."

"Larry, you might as well let them in because the Lord's gonna do what He's gonna do," Lucky called out behind me.

Reluctantly, I opened the door wide. "All right. Come in."

The patrolmen entered, quietly stepping as if they did not want to disturb a sleeping child. They looked around, squinting, their eyes slowly adjusting from the summer brightness to the dim light of the living room.

"Where's the body?" Pedroza voice was still quietly professional.

"In the bedroom."

The officer's unoffensive attitude was giving me fewer reasons to resist.

"May I go there?"

"This way. . . ." As I led him through the living room, I glanced at Lucky. The other officer waited as we disappeared down the hallway and into the bedroom. Wess was lying in the same position as when he died: right knee bent, the leg lifted up from the bed, his head tilted back, mouth slightly open, arms folded over his abdomen, eyes closed. Pedroza approached the bed and began a cursory examination of the body. As he leaned over and placed his ear to Wesley's chest, I was reminded of my brother, who had done the same thing only a little while before.

"May I use your telephone?" Pedroza's question shot through me like an arrow. I led him into the dining room and pointed.

"There it is. What are you going to do—call a back up?"

Pedroza nodded and began to dial. Visions of police swarming all over our house made me uneasy. Lucky sat in the living room shaking and bewildered. "Lord, if You're going to raise Wesley up, please hurry and do it," she prayed silently. "Lord, give me peace in this situation."

Finishing his call, Pedroza asked for more details on Wesley's death.

"He died of sugar diabetes," I began.

"Sugar diabetes? How do you know?"

"Well, he had sugar diabetes, and we were praying for him to be healed."

"Was he on insulin?"

"Yes, but we haven't been giving him insulin. We were praying for him to be healed."

The officer's eyebrows arched slightly. Courteously, he said, "We don't want anyone to leave the house right now. . . ."

A knock on the door interrupted him. Two plain-clothed policemen waited patiently as I opened the door. At their request, I led them into the bedroom. They took pictures of Wesley and searched the rest of the house.

"You're not under arrest, but we will need to question all of you," Detective William Grayer intoned, walking into the living room. "We'd like you to go down to the police station. Mr. and Mrs. Parker, you can go now or wait for the coroner to remove the body."

The look of fright was plain on Lucky's face.

"No," I offered. "We can go . . . now."

"We'll drive you down, Larry," Joyce suggested.

Neighbors were milling about our front yard and driveway, attracted by the police cars parked in front of our home. Most notable among the crowd was Pastor Nash, who looked as if he had just arrived. Walking up the drive to the house, he stopped and stared as we opened the doors of Joyce's car and slipped in. I spotted Karl Kessler in the crowd and nodded apprehensively as we began to pull away. He waved back, smiling weakly.

Sitting in the back seat alone, Lucky and I held hands tightly. "Larry, I'm so nervous. . . ."

"Everything's going to be all right."

"But do you think they'll put us in jail?"

Lucky's voice was rising in panic. she was squeezing my hand so tightly that her knuckles were white. Peeling her hand from mine, I put my arm around her shoulders in comfort.

"Let's just commit this to the Lord. It's all for His glory anyway. He's going to raise Wesley up. Let's ask God for peace."

As I prayed Lucky's shoulders relaxed, and a peaceful calm overtook my body, too. By the time we reached the station, Lucky was so relaxed that someone remarked, "Look at her; she looks like she's had a tranquilizer."

We had been sitting in the front lobby for several minutes when Pastor Nash burst through the glass front doors, stopped abruptly as he angrily scanned the large lobby with his eyes and, seeing Lucky and me, strode over to tower above us. Sharon, Joyce, and Cindy stared at him, eyes wide. Lucky kept her attention on the Bible opened on her lap.

Our pastor's entrance surprised me. I glanced quickly up at the large wall clock opposite the entrance. *It's seven-fifteen. The Wednesday evening service has started. What's he doin' here?*

"Do you realize what you've done?" he demanded, jabbing his finger at all of us. My mind closed shut like a steel trap. I didn't want to hear what he had to say.

"You're all wrong. You've brought a reproach upon the name of Christ. And God's *not* going to bring Wesley back from the dead."

"When he does, then you'll have to apologize," I snapped.

"If that happens, I *will*!" he shouted.

"I don't believe you. I don't wanna hear it . . . I don't wanna hear it. If you can't say anything kind, I don't wanna listen to you. Just go. Leave!" Lucky yelled, clapping her hands over her ears while Pastor Nash continued his tirade.

I was aghast at his anger. If he really believed Wesley wasn't coming back, then he should have felt sympathy for us. Today, however, we realize the embarrassing position in which we had put him and our church.

Pastor Nash stomped out of the station just as Detective Grayer approached.

"Mr. Parker? Could you come with me, please?"

I rose from my seat and followed him to a small cubicle of a room, where I sat down by his desk. After giving my statement, I returned to where Lucky and the other women had been sitting. Sharon and Cindy were not there—"Questioned and driven home," Lucky explained—and Joyce was being interviewed in another cubicle.

The detective who had interrogated me motioned for Lucky to follow him. "Mr. Parker, this won't take long. I'll drive you home after this. We should be done about . . . ." He checked his watch. ". . . oh, ten o'clock. Okay?"

I nodded and sat down on the pew-like bench, watching her disappear into the little room. A man in a business suit sat down next to me.

"Mr. Parker?" he asked, extending his hand.

"I'm the deputy coroner here in Barstow, George Reynolds. I just wanted to tell you that we removed your son's body from the house to the O'Donnell Funeral Home for examination . . . ."

"You mean an autopsy?" A chill shot through me as I thought of a sharp scalpel cutting my son's body, curious eyes and hands prodding him.

"It's just procedure. We need to examine the body to determine cause of death. Your son was a diabetic?"

"Yes."

"And he just deteriorated, right? You *were* administering insulin?"

"No."

The coroner's eyes widened.

"We believe that our son was healed and didn't need it. We've been praying . . . ."

"Are you a Christian?"

"Yes. We attend Calvary Christian Center."

"I'm familiar with that church. I'm a Christian, too." Reynolds smiled.

The tension that had built up in my chest that evening gushed out, and I again felt peaceful. He was a brother in Christ.

". . . and I believe that God heals. I've seen Him work miracles, but I can't believe that you would take your son off medication." He seemed to stare right through me as he spoke. I wondered if anyone would understand. "You don't seem to be grieving much," he finally observed. "Most people I come in contact with would be overcome with sorrow."

He paused for my response.

"Well, we believe Wesley is going to be raised from the dead."

"Raised from the *dead?*" he echoed. "How do you know God's going to do *that?*"

"We just believe it."

"But what if He doesn't?"

"There is no 'if He doesn't . . .' He will. I know it."

"Incredible," he whispered, focusing on me as if I were a strange spiritual phenomenon. He shook his head and changed the subject.

"Will you want his body embalmed?"

I thought for a moment. An autopsy was bad enough, and we probably could do nothing to prevent that. But embalming? The thought of them removing Wesley's blood to replace it with fluid was repulsive.

"No, I don't think that will be necessary."

"In light of your beliefs, I'm not surprised," Reynolds shrugged, rising from the bench to shake my hand.

As we lay in bed that night, each of us wrapped in our own uneasy thoughts, the loneliness of the empty house began to close in. Lucky and I wondered why Grayer asked for Wesley's unused syringes when he drove us home. I had planned to take them to Loma Linda Hospital, where they could be put to use. *Does he want the syringes for evidence?* I shook my head. *Evidence of what?*

6

Perhaps from
the Grave

My eyes flew open when the phone jangled me out of my light sleep. For just a moment I let the Thursday morning light streaming through the bedroom window stab the slumber from my eyes. *The phone, answer the phone.* I fumbled for the phone on the nightstand, grabbed up the receiver and cleared my throat.

"H-hello?"

"Mr. Parker?" the kindly, unfamiliar voice spoke.

"Yes, this is Larry Parker."

It was O'Donnell Mortuary calling to make funeral arrangements. Realizing we would have to go along with the established order despite our belief in Wesley's imminent resurrection, I reluctantly agreed to an appointment for that afternoon.

Slowly hanging up the phone, my mind formulated a plan. *A funeral? No! We'll have a resurrection service!* A knock on the door arrested my attention. *Who could that be, this time of the morning?*

I bounded out of bed, hurriedly pulled on my trousers, and answered the door. Joni Kessler and Christine Dole pushed passed me with a mumbled "good morning" and found their way into our bedroom unannounced, obviously distraught. Still in bed, Lucky sat up with a start.

"Hey, it's okay. I'm all right," she smiled courteously as the women cried and tried to comfort her. Joni and Christine gazed at each other as if to say, "Poor dear, she doesn't realize what happened."

The women were a little worried because Eugene Wilson had told his sister-in-law, Cindy, and Joyce Bannister that we could all be arrested for going along with what had been done.

Trying to make things easier for us, Joni suggested that the children stay with her and Karl tonight instead of coming home from Karen and Eugene's as planned. Neighbors were still jumpy over the events of the past few days, so we agreed. Lucky called Karen about the change in plans just before we left for the mortuary that afternoon. She sounded relieved. We would go to the Wilson's as soon as we were finished with the service arrangements and tell the girls about Wesley.

Sitting in the comfortable, air-conditioned office, waiting for the undertaker to come in for our appointment, we had time to reflect. What should we tell him? What kind of arrangements should we make?

The mortician smiled kindly as he suddenly breezed into his office and sat down smoothly behind his desk. His greeting exhibited the qualities I had noticed in most undertakers. They were professional soothers, men trained to give comfort to the bereaved while taking care of this extensive and expensive business of death and entombment. I had a grudging respect for the profession.

"I'm so sorry about your son's passing. I understand he was a good Christian boy?" His arched eyebrows conveyed a sincerity that I could not deny.

"Yes," Lucky sighed.

shoes to the service."

Quickly changing the subject, the mortician leaned back in his chair. "Well, we need to print up funeral announcements," he offered.

"We don't want any announcements to say 'funeral'. Announce it as a resurrection service!" Lucky suggested.

The man glared at her, glanced at me, and shrugged.

"Okay. Who will be officiating the 'resurrection' service?"

Lucky left the decision to me. Knowing that Pastor Nash wouldn't do it, I thought for a moment. "Let's just say the Holy Spirit."

The man kept writing. "Okay. When?" He had given up trying to be conventional; his professional demeanor was slipping.

"Let's have it Sunday," Lucky suggested.

"Two o'clock okay?" he asked.

"Sure."

Driving to the Wilson's to pick up our children, we pondered how to break the news. I felt tranquil as we pulled up to Eugene's and Karen's home. She answered the door with a worried look on her face.

"Larry . . . Lucky. Hi . . . come in. The girls are across the street watching T.V.," she smiled nervously. "Jay's asleep in my bedroom."

"Isn't Eugene here, Karen?"

"No, he's working his shift today."

"Oh. I was hoping he would be here to pray with us. We wanted to tell the children what happened yesterday, so they won't hear it from someone else. Will you pray with us that they'll understand what happened, and why we are doing what we're doing?"

Karen nodded. Robin Clark, the neighbor from across the street, also was present. Standing in a circle in Karen's living room, we joined hands and prayed. "Lord, give us the words to say that our children will understand. . . ."

When we finished, Robin went to get Pam and Patsy. Peering through Karen's front window at Robin's house, I watched the girls bound out of the front door, stop at the curb to look for traffic, then run across the street and up the driveway, breathless and excited.

"Hi, Mom, Dad!" they called, bursting into the living room. They ran up and hugged me, then Lucky who had made herself comfortable in one of Karen's overstuffed chairs. The three of them giggled and hugged as I slowly sank onto the couch nearby.

"Girls, we have something important to tell you," I began carefully, not wanting to come right out and tell them that their big brother had died. "Wesley . . ." I looked at Lucky. She smiled, and gave a small nod. ". . . Wess has gone to Heaven for a little while, but he's coming back."

"You mean he's with Jesus?" Patsy asked.

I breathed a sigh of half-relief. "Yes. He's with Jesus."

"Oh," Pam stamped and pouted, "that lucky stiff!"

Lucky and I grinned at each other. Soon all four of us were hugging and smiling together at Pam's poor choice of words.

Suddenly, Pam straightened up and stood apart from us. "Is that all you wanted to tell us?"

"Uh, yes, that's all," Lucky smiled, looking at me as she spoke. "I guess. Honey?"

"Yeah, kids. That's all."

"Could we go back and watch T.V. across the street? There was a really good show on. . . ."

"Sure, go ahead."

Pam took off through the front door like a shot while Pat struggled to her feet and ran in hot pursuit. As I watched them run down the driveway, Karen spoke. I had forgotten that she was there.

"I'm amazed," she observed softly, looking out the front window. "Unbelievable." She focused her attention on us. "Praise the Lord! He answered our prayer —they understand."

Robin walked through the front door at that moment, shaking her head in disbelief. "I don't believe your kids," she laughed. "They're over there telling mine that their brother is with Jesus, and they're not even upset. My kids asked whether it bothered them that Wess was dead. Know what they said? 'No! We're expecting him to come back!' " She turned to look out through Karen's open doorway to her house. "Amazing. . . ."

Lucky and I attended a prayer meeting that evening. We had taken the children to the Kesslers and Karl invited us to the meeting. It was to be held at the home of Mardi Clay, who lived nearby.

As Lucky and I walked into Mardi's home, we were immediately besieged by attention. Karl introduced us. "Hey, everybody—this is Larry and Lucky Parker, the ones whose son died yesterday. We're going to pray tonight that the Lord will raise him up." The attention of the fifteen or so people there shifted to us. "Do you want to say anything, Larry?" Karl smiled expectantly.

As I recounted the last three days—the agonizing

times of prayer, the sleepless nights, our house being searched by the police, the questioning at the police station, our experience with the mortician—the people listened intently. Then we all began to pray, asking for the safety of our children and for the glorious resurrection of Wesley's body. The meeting lasted more than two hours.

After it was over, Mardi invited us to spend the night. "It must be awfully lonely over at your house, without Wesley and the kids, and the neighbors staring and curious," she observed. "You'll be close to the children here, since Karl and Joni live in this area." We accepted, gratefully.

On the next day, Friday, the news broke about what we had done. The investigation gave rise to stories that factually told of our striving in prayer for Wesley's healing and resurrection, and horror stories that depicted us as members of an off-beat cult. The newsmen who had called that morning at our home all seemed to be seeking the truth. I told them everything I knew, thinking it was good that the media was in on this, for when the Lord brings Wesley back, there would be no doubt as to his death, and God would get the glory for his resurrection. I didn't realize the diversity that could result from telling the same story to a half-a-dozen different reporters. The San Bernardino paper seemed to report the event accurately, but in the coming days we felt some of the press was out to deliberately sensationalize the truth.

Saturday we went home from Mardi's house to check the mail and to pick up the newspaper from the driveway. There was nothing unusual in the mail, but as I opened the front door, the telephone began to ring.

Finally getting off the phone two hours later, I was exhausted. I had spoken over three live radio talk shows whose hosts wanted to know more about the story, and several other news people, including Regis Philbin. The calls were from all over—Chicago, Northern California, Los Angeles.

"But you sound so happy! Aren't you grieving over your son's death?" they would probe.

"Of course not. I believe without a doubt that God will raise my son from the dead," I would answer.

Leaving the house that day, I smiled grimly—*The Lord's got the word out now—Wesley will rise.*

When we finally pulled into the O'Donnell Funeral Home parking lot that hot Sunday afternoon, it was only one-thirty. The lot was almost full. We had picked up the children from the Kessler's, and had expected that if we arrived this early, we would have plenty of time to ready ourselves for the big moment. We didn't expect to see such a crowd. A lone reporter milling around the entrance spotted us as we headed for the side door of the mortuary.

"May I have a word with you, Mr. Parker?" The reporter fumbled with the tape recorder strapped over his shoulder.

"I only have one word for the press." Raising my Bible as I spoke, I tried to sound cheerful and positive. "My son, Wesley, will be raised from the dead today!"

We brushed past the reporter and entered the chapel, letting the girls scurry inside. Carrying Jay, Lucky walked slowly behind, a smile on her face. An all-pervading warmth flooded my soul as I absently picked up a funeral announcement from the small table placed in the center of the foyer.

The auditorium was jammed to capacity with people awaiting Wesley's return. Some from Mardi's prayer meeting and friends from our church joined us in the family section. I expected to see more members from my church, but Pastor Nash had scheduled a memorial service for Wesley at the same time. We felt deserted.

Some of the faithful had their heads bowed in prayer; others watched us with great hope shining from their eyes. Then there were the curious—the smirking eyes, the sneering lips, the mouths that opened in quiet laughter.

"Oh, God," I prayed, "please honor your servants' prayers today." I wanted desperately to show the world that God was indeed alive—and able to raise the dead. But most of all I wanted my son.

The funeral home had done a good job. Wesley's plain, open casket was laid out on a simple white bench, in front, in full view—the center of attention. No flowers decorated the chapel.

The crowd began to stir impatiently. I glanced at the small announcement in my hand, then opened it to see what was supposed to happen. "Resurrection Service, the Holy Spirit Presiding," it read. *The Holy Spirit!* Suddenly in a panic, I looked around the crowded room at the fidgeting forms, then at my watch. *Quarter after two. Better get started.*

Mardi motioned to a young man who had brought his guitar to begin playing. He strummed the familiar tune, *Amazing Grace,* and we began to sing. Soon the audience joined in the singing.

Amazing grace, how sweet the sound,
That saved a wretch like me. . . .

The words of the hymn were comforting. After a few choruses, I cleared my throat and stood. A hush fell on the chapel, and all eyes focused on me. *This is it! This is when Wesley is supposed to be raised!* Faith abandoned me at that moment. When I opened my mouth to speak, a ton of fear pressed on my shoulders.

"It says in the Gospel of John, chapter eleven," I opened to the silent congregation, ". . . that Jesus raised Lazarus from the grave. And that's what we're here for today—to see the bodily resurrection of Wesley Parker, one of Jesus Christ's own. Just like Lazarus, he will rise." Then I read the passage and asked everyone to pray.

I felt empty and helpless during my prayer. Finished, I opened my eyes and gazed upon the simple casket.

"Wesley," I squeaked, then continued in a stronger, but trembling voice, "Wesley, rise up in the name of Jesus."

Nothing happened.

"Wesley, I command you to rise in Jesus' name."

I gestured for the guitarist to join me in front of the casket. Embarrassed silence permeated the room.

"Jim, let's worship the Lord some more," I whispered.

"Okay." Turning to the crowd, his guitar strapped over his shoulder, he began to sing the familiar hymn, *Tis So Sweet to Trust in Jesus*. The audience joined in after the first few words.

I sat down and worshiped along with the rest. The singing was nearly deafening. I was happy, that there were enough sympathetic people in the crowd to make the singing so loud.

"Larry," someone called from the audience. I did

not turn around, but riveted my attention on the casket. The voice was not familiar. "Larry, I think the Lord wants all of the children to call Wesley back to life."

I stood, motioning to the girls. They dutifully followed as other children joined them around the casket. They prayed silently for several seconds as the audience watched. Then meekly, quietly, they began to call, "Wesley . . . Wesley . . . rise . . . Wesley."

Nothing.

The children repeated the phrase over and over, until I could stand it no longer. I gently guided them toward their chairs. As they sat down, a young man stood up in the center of the chapel and intoned, "The ground upon which you are standing is holy ground." A hush again fell on the audience. *A word from God!* I thought, hopefully. *Should I have everyone remove their shoes? Yes!*

"Just like it says in Exodus," I told the crowd, "when Moses saw the burning bush and heard those very words, we should remove our shoes." My reasoning was simple: Perhaps this was a sign of faith—anyone who did not remove their shoes did not believe and thus was hindering Wesley's resurrection. Slowly walking up and down the aisle, I searched for people who had not taken them off, and politely asked the unbelievers to leave. Soon the chapel was only half-filled—with the faithful and the die-hard curious.

A young man with long hair and a beard walked up to me as Jim led in another song. "Excuse me, Mr. Parker. Would you let me pray with Wesley . . . alone?"

Staring blankly at the youth, I considered his strange request, open to any suggestion at the moment. Then the thought struck me. Perhaps he was an angel sent from God to answer our prayers.

"Yes, of course, go right ahead. Uh, people," I announced, my mind racing with excitement, "I'm going to ask you to please get up quietly and leave. The service is over."

The audience began to file out of the chapel, some muttering in disappointment. "Karl wants to leave now," Joni said. "Do you want us to take the kids with us to get ready for Jay's birthday?" Disappointment for us was deeply etched on her face.

"Whataya think?" Lucky looked up at me.

"Yeah, that's a good idea."

"It's getting late, and we may be here awhile. Pam, why don't you and Patsy go with the Kesslers and Jay. We'll bring Wesley later," Lucky instructed.

"Aw, we want to see him raised," the girls begged.

"No, you go ahead and go with the Kesslers."

As the girls walked through the foyer and into the hot afternoon, Lucky fought back the tears. Tony and Carol kept us company in the foyer as we waited for the young man praying for Wesley's resurrection.

The chapel doors opened suddenly, and the youth emerged slowly from the auditorium. Hope burned in our eyes, then faded, as he met our gaze dejectedly, tears disappearing into his beard. Without a word, he stepped across the lobby and out into the bright sunshine.

Lucky and I sat quietly for a few long minutes, staring at the doors that led into the chapel. We visualized the small, still casket, unmoved, still bearing its precious load.

"I'm sorry, Mr. and Mrs. Parker. It's almost seven, and we have to close," the mortician spoke softly as he approached. "Mr. Parker, would you come with me for a moment?"

I stood and followed him to the business counter, where the mortician asked, "When shall we bury the body? It's required by the law after. . . ."

"All right . . . we'll . . . go ahead and bury him, then. But don't tell the reporters when you go, and don't allow anyone to go with you."

Burial seemed too final. It was all I could do to hang on to my belief that God was going to bring Wesley back. I just couldn't commit him to the ground. Attending the burial would have been an admission that all hope was gone. I couldn't accept that.

Out of the corner of my eye, I saw the reporter approaching. "What now, Mr. Parker? Your son *did not* rise," he probed kindly.

"It's just like Lazarus when he was raised from the grave," I countered. "He laid in the grave for four days. We'll allow Wesley to be buried; and then God will raise him up after four days. That's what's going to happen."

To avoid the newsman, Lucky had slipped out the front entrance. Now I joined her outside. The reporter followed.

"Do you have anything to say, Mrs. Parker?"

Lucky just shook her head as we walked away.

Jay's second birthday party was subdued. The girls had expected Wesley to walk through the door with us and were crushed when he didn't. Too young to understand, Jay happily blew out the two candles on his cake. Devastated with disappointment, Lucky could not even go through the motions of a celebration as were the others. She stayed in the living room at the

Kessler's trying to compose herself for the children's sake. Pam and Patsy looked at each other with moist eyes as they heard their mother's stifled sobs from the other room.

Although my heart was heavy with grief, I was numb and unable to weep, still holding on to those hopeful Bible verses about Jesus and Lazarus.

We left Jay's party and headed for Mardi's home, where we were staying. The girls looked forlorn as they hugged us goodbye. We wanted desperately to be with them, but there wasn't enough room at either house for all of us. Once in the car, a dangerous suggestion entered my mind. *What you ought to do*, it advised, *is call those reporters and tell them that if Wesley isn't raised from the dead in four days, then there is no God*.

Immediately I recognized this as coming from Satan and rejected the intruding thought. Inwardly I had begun to admit to the prospect that Wesley might not come back. *Even if it doesn't happen*, I mused, *I will not turn my back on God. I will not accuse Him of failing us*. A deep fatigue settled on me then, dulling my mind. I gave up trying to figure it all out.

The desert sunset was settling into its beautiful reds and yellows, splashing the dusty mountains to the east with purplish shades of color as we pulled into Mardi's drive. The loneliness we felt is only partly expressed in the poignant *Los Angeles Times* story of his burial.

"BARSTOW—Wesley Parker, age 11, is buried in Mountain View Cemetery. It is late afternoon before the wind picks up and takes its razor licks at the trees, and the shade finally slides across his grave. The sod, which had turned yellow when it was replaced, is beginning to take hold and grow green again. . . .

"Mountain View Cemetery is on the other side of

town. It is a hopeful place, a verdant square planted with trees. The green ends at the fence line, where the daily irrigations give way to the Mojave's pink and greyish brown colored rock, shimmering into the distance. The cemetery says a lot about Barstow, an optimistic town strung out along route 66 and the Santa Fe Railroad, where 18,000 residents hope that a nation of travelers will stop long enough to buy some gas, food, or a night's rest.

". . . After three days without insulin, Wesley Parker died. His father and mother, faith unshaken and Bibles clutched to their hearts, arranged for a special service in a local funeral parlor where, they predicted, God would raise Wesley from the dead and send him out to walk among men and teach the glory of the Word.

"Wesley did not rise. On the following morning, the undertaker, following directions from Wesley's father, took the body to the cemetery and, in the company of a gravedigger and the cemetery manager, committed Wesley Parker to the ground without a prayer. . . ."[1]

1. Excerpted from "Wesley Parker and the Will of God—A Test of Faith in an Apocalyptic Setting," Charles T. Powers, *Los Angeles Times*, Sept. 14, 1973.

7

"Why Has God Forsaken Us?"

"Mr. Parker, we've investigated your son's death, and have come to place you and your wife under arrest!"

The officer looked at a small card in his hand and began to read: "You have the absolute right to remain silent. Anything you say can and will be used against you in a court of law. . . ."

Like the fury of fire, the agony of those words burned into my heart. It was Wednesday, August 29.

One week had passed since Wesley's death, and we were awaiting his resurrection, which I believed would occur the next day. I had been sitting in our living room, relaxing, reading the mail. Lucky was writing a letter to her mother. Gazing outside to gather her thoughts, Lucky's face had suddenly frowned with curiosity.

"Larry! Look outside. What's happening?"

Several police units had pulled up in front of our house. Detective Grayer had just emerged from an unmarked vehicle and was walking briskly up our driveway toward the front door, several uniformed patrolmen close behind him.

Now as he read me my rights through the screen door, words gurgled silently in my throat as I tried to speak. I felt Lucky's eyes staring at my back. A gaggle of reporters and T.V. cameramen were running down the sidewalk and across our lawn hoping to get their cameras into position to capture the arrest.

"Do you understand your rights, Mr. Parker?"

"Yes."

"Mrs. Parker?"

"I guess so."

"I'll read it again, Mrs. Parker."

"No . . . that's all right. I understand."

"Uh, well, do you mind if I get my Bible?" I looked into Grayer's eyes, pleading after he had finished.

"All right, you can go get your Bible." He was firm, but gentle.

I shuffled to the coffee table and picked it up.

"Mr. Grayer, I just wrote a letter to my mother," Lucky said. "Could you give me a moment to address it and go into the bedroom to get my purse?"

"Yes, if you'll hurry."

Returning from the bedroom, Lucky addressed the envelope, inserted the letter and sealed it.

"Would you mail this for me?" she asked handing him the letter.

"Yes, Ma'am."

Her face a mask, frozen emotionless, she stopped next to the light stand near the front door, bent stiffly, and picked up a small Bible—it had been Wesley's. I opened the screen, and we stepped out into the sweltering heat.

The cameras began to click-whir-click-whir-click as we were handcuffed, the cold, hard bite of the steel clamps a foreboding shadow of events to come. The evening news would show the action.

Aroused by the swarm of officers and reporters, our

neighbors were out in force—some were gawking, craning their necks to see what was happening at the 'kooks' house on their block; others stood back, faces grim, arms folded across their chests as if to say, "Serves 'em right!"

Officer Grayer led Lucky to a policewoman who escorted her to a patrol unit.

"C'mon, Mr. Parker, let's go," one of the uniformed officers ordered. The gawking crowd, the whirring T.V. cameras, and the bustling media created an atmosphere of excitement as we walked silently to the patrol car down the street.

With my wrists twisted in the loosely clasped handcuffs as we drove to the Barstow city jail, I comforted myself with the idea that we were being persecuted for our faith.

There was little time for me to think while sitting in the holding cell. It was tiny—just a little room with dull green walls, a large steel door with a small, shatterproof window, a small wooden chair in the middle of the room. Glad that my handcuffs had been removed, I rubbed my wrists consolingly.

"Let's go, Parker," an officer growled as he abruptly opened the steel door to my cell. I was beginning to resent being treated like a criminal. Yet, to these men in uniform, I *was*. Their demeanor was always the same—gruff, but not mean, abrupt in their commands and actions.

I stepped responsively to the commands of this man, eventually finding myself in an interrogation room similar to the one in which I was questioned on the evening of Wesley's death.

Detective Grayer walked briskly into the room and

sat down across from me at a desk in the center. "I need to ask you a few more questions about last Wednesday, Mr. Parker. We found a few discrepancies in yours and Mrs. Parker's statements. . . ."

As Grayer questioned me further, his demeanor was more intense, like a bloodhound sniffing out a trail.

"Will I be able to see my wife soon?" I asked meekly.

"Oh, yes . . . In fact, we're going to take you both over to the Sheriff's station across the street for booking. I should tell you now—you'll be booked for murder." The detective paused, observing my obvious shocked reaction.

Murder! I gulped. *But how can they?*

"Of course, that's just a preliminary charge," he reassured. "They'll get down to a specific charge at your arraignment—like what degree, or if it's manslaughter. Nothing you can do, except wait."

He escorted me back to the holding cell, where moments later a uniformed officer produced handcuffs, and again I was in bonds. He and Grayer ushered me down the hall to the large, glass back door of the police station. Lucky was waiting, handcuffed, with a matron. The expression on her face was strained and frightened. Later I learned why.

Her holding tank was filthy. It was dark, a dim light reflecting through a tiny window about six inches square. Her only furnishings were a metal bunk bed and a dirty urinal. The cell at the Sheriff's station was decent, but the one at the city jail wasn't fit for a rat, even though the facility was fairly new.

"Empty your pockets, Parker," the booking deputy at the San Bernardino County Sheriff's Station ordered. He was seated at a desk, and I stood like a lug in front of him, hesitating.

"I said, emp-ty your pock-ets," he sneered.

Out came my wallet, change, keys—onto the desk.

"Now, I want you to take off your belt, your ring there, and your watch."

He counted the dollar bills inside my wallet, then recorded the amount on a large manila envelope on which he had written my name and the date. He scooped my belt, ring, and watch along with the wallet into the envelope and began to seal it when he spied my Bible sitting on the edge of his desk. As he reached for it, I spoke for the first time.

"Uh, please, sir," I coughed. He looked up in mock surprise.

"Well, what is it?" he snapped, a look of rigid authority clamping down his eyebrows like slamming barred windows. He held my precious Bible in his hand, poised at the open mouth of the envelope.

"Well, I was wondering if I could keep my Bible. It would mean a lot to me."

"Why not," he shrugged, leafing through the thin pages and taking loose papers out of it. The deputy slid my notes into the envelope, sealed it, and set it aside. Handing me the Bible, he rose from the seat. "Here you go; now, follow me."

Soon I was in an open-bar cell with three other men. The prisoners stared, sizing me up.

"Oh, Jesus," I prayed silently, "don't let them start anything. The way I feel, I'm liable to lash out at them, and that wouldn't be right." I plopped down on the nearest bunk, trying to ignore them.

"Hey! Who said you could have that one?" snapped the one in the T-shirt and tan slacks. Turning toward him, I glared straight into his eyes and snarled.

"I did!"

"Okay, if you feel that way about it," he muttered.

"He's a bank robber," piped one of the others.

They ignored me after that, each lost in his own lonely thoughts. Later, after a tasteless T.V. dinner, a big, burly deputy jerked open the bars with a loud squeak.

"Okay . . . Parker, you come with me."

I quickly walked to stand in front of the deputy, half-in, half-out of the cell, uncertain of my next move.

"C'mon," he snapped, giving my shoulder a little push.

"What's happening?" I asked, confused.

The officer locked the cell and slowly turned on his heels to face me, his arms raised, hands on hips. Jutting his chin out, his eyes narrowed, "We're gonna take you to County Jail. Down in San Berdoo. Let's go!"

We walked briskly to where I had been booked, fingerprinted and photographed. Lucky was waiting. Deputies gave us both the envelopes in which our valuables were kept and handcuffed us. I glanced up at the wall clock above the booking desk. *Eight o'clock.* Hands in authority pulled us toward the back door of the station. The closed in feeling, the still, stale air, the unannounced clangs of cell doors closing, the muffled complaints of the prisoners: These things made our stay seem like forever.

As they led us into the desert dusk, where the air was fresh and clear, the sky wide open and free, I took a deep breath. How I appreciated the desert, with its subtle changes of color as the sun went down in the west. I stared out of the car window at the Joshua trees, the scrub brush and sand, watching the setting sun play with their lengthening shadows. The mountains appeared low, spiny as the backs of prehistoric lizards. The open spaces leading to the rocky, barren hills were changing colors from tan to brown to red.

The handcuffs on my wrists suddenly became unbearably confining. I turned to look at Lucky. She had been observing me with her deep, forlorn eyes, wondering what I was thinking. We had driven well past Victorville by now, and had just begun our descent from the high desert, through the Cajon Pass, and into San Bernardino.

I was astounded at the immensity of the San Bernardino County Jail. Again, we were separated. For how long, neither of us could guess. A day, a week, a month? Years? I shuddered to think of Lucky in a lonely cell, quietly driven mad.

After my valuables were examined for a second time, I was ordered to undress. I did, and was led to a room where I was mechanically showered and deliced. My jailers then gave me a pair of orange, ill-fitting, long sleeved coveralls, with the letter "P" silkscreened on the back.

P for prisoner, I winced. *I'm a prisoner. Oh, God, why am I going through this?*

Laden with a blanket and sheets, I was told to follow a deputy to my cell. I prayed that I'd be alone.

"So you're Parker, eh?" My escort sounded warmer than his colleagues, not sarcastic,

"Uh, yes." I felt like extending my hand for a handshake, but mentally withdrew as we strolled along the catwalk lined with open bar cells.

"You're the one who prayed for his son to be healed and then let him die?"

A defensive feeling swelled in my chest. "Well, he'll be raised up tomorrow, out of the grave."

"Just like Lazarus?"

"Well, yeah."

"You know, I attend a church here in San Bernardino. You've caused kind of a ruckus in our congregation—some people are saying that you were arrested for your faith."

This man was a Christian. Perhaps I could express my true feelings.

"Now I know how Paul the Apostle felt when he was arrested," I smiled comfortably.

The deputy stopped, turned, and stared me straight in the eye. "Yeah, but Paul was put into prison for doing the *Lord's* work."

Already feeling judged and condemned, my heart sank once more. The look in his eye, and the way he abruptly turned and resumed walking down the catwalk toward my cell, confirmed what Lucky and I had come to realize. Except for a few friends, we stood alone in the Christian community. That prejudice cut through my heart like a knife.

We proceeded silently down a small flight of stairs to a group of tiny cells. He opened the solid-looking steel door of one and motioned me inside. On the door a small painted plaque read "Suicidal." I had just enough light from the outside shining through the window set in the upper middle of the door to see my quarters. There was barely enough room to stand next to the bunk in front of a commode, above it a sink with a metal mirror.

After a quick glance around the bedsize room, I peered through the window. The deputy had left. I recalled the word "Suicidal" on the outside of the door.

Being in this tiny space would make anyone want to kill himself, I grumbled.

I threw my blanket and sheets onto the bunk, and realized suddenly that there was no pillow. With a sigh, I crawled onto the bunk, moving as far to the head, and as far away from the steel door and its window, as possible. Lying on my side, I curled my legs up to my chest, thankful to be alone, and dozed. . . .

Suddenly, the door opened with the sound of metal scraping metal. The light bulb inside the cubicle snapped on, stabbing my eyes with pain.

"So this is the child-killing devil . . ." the guard sneered viciously. "You are the lowest. . . ." It was after midnight and the changing of the guard. This officer worked himself into a frenzy of hatred, cursing me over and over as I laid there not knowing what to do. He finally slammed the door with a loud clang, and stormed off, leaving the light on in the cell.

The glare prevented even the lightest of sleep. And every half-hour or so the guard would peek through the window, beat the door with his fists, hurl epitaphs, and call me "child-killer." Strangely, I felt no fear, only pity for this man. He couldn't possibly understand the circumstances surrounding my arrest.

During those moments of harassment, I felt so far from God. "Holy Spirit, You're the Comforter—comfort me. And Lucky. Please, Holy Spirit. . . ."

I was aroused in the early morning by a light knock. I mused about the silliness of that knocking—did my visitor expect me to open the door for him? With the rattle of keys, a man dressed in plain clothes opened the cell and spoke. "I'm the staff psychiatrist. How was your night?"

Of course! Who else would they send to a cell for

suicidal maniacs? "Fine," I smiled faintly. "I'm okay. How's my wife? Is she okay? Can you get a message to her?"

"You'll see her soon enough. You're going back to Barstow for arraignment in a few minutes. I just wanted to see how you were."

I stared at the plate glass pane after he left, a glimmer of hope in my eyes. At least I could get out of this horrible place—even for a few hours. *How can people stand to be shut up like this?*

Even though we were cuffed and chained in the back of the patrol car, Lucky practically clung to me the entire distance between San Bernardino and Barstow. Her night had been equally distressing. She had been taken from holding cell to holding cell, then made to strip and shower. Humiliated by the ever watchful eyes of the matrons, she was doused with delicing powder and given a straight denim dress. She, too, had been put in a tiny "Suicidal" cell. The close confinement made her want to scream.

"But the worst thing was that I didn't even think that Jesus cared for me," Lucky cried as she described her experiences. "I had my Bible and tried to read it, but I just couldn't. I tried to pray, but I couldn't. It didn't feel as if He was anywhere around."

I patted her knee in comfort, but the clinking of the chains around my wrists served only to drive me further into an uncomfortable state of mind. *Had* God forsaken us? Were we *truly* alone, without friends or God? I peered out over the upper desert plain as we rode. *Even the desert has its plants, mountains, and the stars and moon at night to keep it company.*

We arrived in Barstow about noon. After waiting in

separate holding tanks in the Sheriff's station, we were taken across a gully to the courthouse. The press was there taking pictures and asking questions. In the small courtroom we learned our charges: Involuntary manslaughter and felony child abuse. Our bail was set at ten thousand dollars each. Without work or money for bail, we were declared indigent, which meant that we had to stay in jail. That gave us the right to a court-appointed attorney, a public defender. *A mixed blessing,* I thought wryly.

On our trip back to San Bernardino, we were cuffed to the chains around our waists again. Although we appeared calm, the rejection we felt from some of our family, church, and friends added to our anxiety. What would we face back in jail?

It was bad enough that the Lord took Wesley, but why did we have to go through this? Perhaps, because of what we did, we'd never see our other children again. Would they be raised by someone else? Would they remember us when we got out of prison—especially Jay because he was so little? Lucky and I had faced the prospects of not seeing each other again as well.

In her cell the night before, Lucky had wrestled with her anger at God. She had wanted to say, "Hey, Jesus—if that's the way it is, then just leave me. I don't want any part of You." But as she was trying to say those words, the Holy Spirit seemed to seal her lips. She would have rejected the Lord, but the Spirit showed her in a gentle way that Jesus was her only hope.

8

Did We Make a Mistake?

"C'mon, Parker, we've got a cell for you in the housing section," a guard's voice barked through the thick door of my holding tank.

Lucky and I had been separated again after our arraignment and returned to county jail, chained and cuffed back into that monolithic dungeon of stone and metal. With body once again in a small, dimly-lit cell, my mind sank—falling, swirling into the abyss of depression. My only link to hope was the Bible that I still clutched.

Hardly before the jailer announced the change in cells, the door opened, light from the bright hallway pouring in, shrinking and shoving my depression to the back of my skull. My spirits began to lift as we walked upstairs instead of down. After passing through several lockups—barred doors separating one section of the jail from the other—I was placed in a cell away from the main group, reserved for prisoners who needed protection from hostile inmates. It was a two-man abode, with a wash basin and mirror, a metal desk and stool attached to the wall, a toilet, and an upper and lower bunk. I was alone with a world of room, compared to the previous night's accommodation. I stood in the middle of the cell, hands on my hips, and nodded to no one in particular, *Now this is a bit more livable. At least I have a little room to move around.*

My escort was standing in front of the bars, observing me. I felt like a caged zoo animal under his sneering gaze.

"Heard you had your bail set at ten thousand bucks. At that amount, you'll *never* get out." His mouth broke into an evil grin as he turned to walk away. "Never!" he called back.

Later I was given a pencil, which I used to draw a small calendar on the back page of my Bible. The scene was similar to that in the movie about the count of Monte Cristo. He had drawn a calendar also. As the days crawled by I would cross out the dates on the calendar.

I noticed the sounds of the jail much more than on my first night: The loud television in the dayroom continually shouting its advertising, the constant steps in the hallways and on the catwalks—guards leading prisoners to and from the dayroom, the visitation room, the shower room—the endless clanging of barred doors in a staccato-like rhythm—slam, slam, slam, slam. No wonder jails are known by one of their more popular nicknames: the slammer. These noises only caused my anxiety to grow. At first alarmed at the clatter, I would jump up to investigate the noises nearest me, only to look upon a long row of monotonous, bright yellow bars. Within a few hours, my alarm had subsided to simple irritation. But the anxiety created by this relentless racket, and the circumstances in which I found myself, kept me diligent in my prayers.

"Holy Spirit," I would plead, "comfort me. Comfort me and Lucky."

Occasionally an opportunity arose for me to talk with the men in my section. Most of the time, the four of us kept to ourselves, reading, thinking, counting the cinder blocks on the wall opposite the cells. One, a man named Ben Halstead, was in the cell next to me. Through a guard, he had given me the pencil and later some paper, which I used in writing a letter to Lucky. Through this initial contact, I discovered that Ben was a warm, tenderhearted person, although neither of us were eager to share the reasons for our confinement.

Passing his cell one morning on the way back from a shower, I saw Ben sitting on his bunk reading a red-covered paperback book. When he turned a page, I caught a glimpse of the cover. It was Hal Lindsey's *The Late Great Planet Earth.* How I had loved that book! It had shown me how little time we have until our Lord's return, and it had been a stimulating force in my boldness to tell people about Christ. I stood there in sorrow, realizing that I was in no position to tell this man about Jesus.

"Lord, I can't testify to this man. I can't tell him about You. I'm so confused myself. Lord—please, would You use that book to reach him?"

The next day, a guard escorted me to the dayroom. The television was blaring away—the show "M.A.S.H.," a new program that was based upon the movie about a hospital unit stationed in Korea during the Korean War. Several men were gathered around the set, staring blankly at the screen, their minds soaking up anything, anything that would take them far away from the monotonous life of a cell. Ben was there, too, but his expression was different. His face brightened by the humor, he grinned broadly, occasionally chuckling. Released from the custody of the guard, I drifted into the room and sat next to him. The book he was reading was in his lap. During a commercial, I jabbed my thumb toward it and cautiously asked, "Hey, Ben, did you finish it yet?"

He looked surprised. "Uh, yeah. Yeah, I did."

"What didja think of it?"

"It was, uh, good." The look of calm, relaxed joy on his face faded into one of suspicion.

"Did you enjoy it?"

"Yes, I did. Why?"

"Did it affect you in any way?" I smiled, and then explained, "I'm curious, because, well, I read it too, and I'm . . . a Christian." Blood shot through to my temples when I said this, causing my face to burn red.

Ben relaxed, a nervous smile flickering on his face. "Well, it did affect me." He looked down and fingered the book. "It affected me a lot. It really pulled everything together—it all made so much sense—and, well, it asked me if I wanted to accept Christ as my Savior. . . ." His voice had dropped to a whisper as he spoke. He paused for a reflective moment. I was at the edge of my seat as he slapped the paperback on his knee and announced, ". . . and I did!" Ben looked at me, a glow of victory shining from his eyes.

One day a guard shoved a tray of food through a horizontal slit in the bars, made just for that purpose. Somehow I couldn't eat it. *Maybe I should fast*, I thought. After turning away a few meals, I sensed that my jailers were displeased.

"Lord, if you want me to fast, I don't care what the jailers think. But if this is not Your will for me now, show me," I prayed. "When they bring the next meal, I'll taste it. If You want me to continue fasting, make it taste bad. That shouldn't be hard in this place."

I didn't have long to wait. In the upper left corner of the metal dinner tray was a horrible looking brown slop. *Probably mashed sweet potato. Never did like the stuff. I'll taste that.* Dipping my spoon into the ugly mess, I brought it to my lips. The Lord answered my prayer, but not in the way that I had expected. It had a delicious, sweet, pumpkin pie flavor. I ate it all. Later I would learn how important it was not to continue my fast.

"Hey, Parker—you've got a visitor. C'mon. . . ." the guard said gruffly, abruptly opening my cell. It protested with a sliding screech. I hesitated on my bunk, wondering who would want to visit me.

"C'mon, move it," the guard snapped.

Grabbing my Bible as I walked into the barred corridor, I flipped to the page with the calendar. It was Saturday. My heart glowed with the happy prospect of seeing a visitor as we walked haltingly through the lockups toward the visitation cubicle.

"This way, Parker." The guard motioned toward the seat in front of the waist high shelf that protruded from the cubicle wall. A thick plate glass partition separated prisoner from visitor. I could clearly see the auburn-haired man awaiting me.

"Pastor Nash!" My face brightened with surprise. We sat silently for a few seconds. He smiled warmly, compassionately.

A flood of despair hit me so suddenly that I began to sob. The agony of my loneliness and the anguish of my experiences combined to make my frustration unbearable.

"P-pastor, what can you do to get us out of here? This is such a terrible place," I spoke through a round screened opening in the glass. "I'm so worried about Lucky and the kids. . . ."

He looked down at his folded hands on the shelf, embarrassed at my sudden outbreak.

"Uh, Larry," he began, his voice deep and soothing. "I'm afraid I can't do anything for you right now. It's Labor Day weekend. . . ," I had forgotten. ". . . and all the agencies dealing with your case are closed. I also have some bad news. . . ."

He looked down at his hands, now clenched into a double fist, relaxed them and looked up again.

"I wish I wasn't the one having to tell you this, but . . . your children have been taken away from the Kessler's by the county and put in Juvenile Hall."

The pastor's shoulders drooped, relieved of their burden. He had said what he had come to say. Taking a deep breath, he raised one eyebrow in a question, watching for my reaction.

I did not react, visibly. My face was frozen into a mask of emotionless mental fatigue. Finally, I said, hollowly, "but why did they pick up the kids?"

He shook his head sorrowfully. "The authorities found out that Karl frowned on the use of medicine, and they were concerned for the safety of the children."

"Couldn't they have let my brother take them?"

"Well, I think they may be working on that, Larry. But they can't do anything until Tuesday."

"Isn't there *anything* you can do to get us out of here?"

Pastor Nash just shrugged with outspread hands.

"Thanks for coming, Pastor." I felt empty inside, totally cheerless. *Well, he's done his duty—like the Bible says, you gotta visit those in prison or. . . . At least I had a chance to get outa my cell for awhile*, I thought bitterly. Then out loud I said, "Goodbye" and signaled for the guard.

It was Monday, two days after Pastor Nash had brought me the bad news about our children, four days since I had seen Lucky, five following our arrest. I was sitting on my bunk, reading the Bible.

"God!" I shouted, snapping the book shut and stomping to my feet. "God . . . God . . ." the cell block echoed, forcing my voice to hush. ". . . when will I get outa here?" I paced up and down the cell, Bible clutched in both hands. My nerves were drawn, tight as a drum head, ready to snap. I kept reviewing in my mind the events of the past few days, again pleading with God for comfort.

Suddenly stopping in the center of the cell, I reached upward with my arms, Bible in hand. "Oh, Lord, when, *how* are we going to get outa here?" A strange thought flashed across my mind:

Patience, son . . . soon.

The words weren't mine. Oddly, they kept echoing through the sinus chambers of my skull—*Patience, son . . . soon.* The message wasn't audible, but it might as well have been. Clearly, they were words of comfort from the Lord. He had heard me!

A warmth began to ooze from the top of my head to the ends of my toes, loosening the uptightness that had bound my body for the last five days. The Comforter was comforting. Again the thought, *Patience, son . . . soon.* Deep within a bubble of joy began to swell.

Early the next morning a trustee stared at me curiously as he slipped my breakfast under the barred door. "By the way, I wouldn't drink that milk; someone spit in it," he warned.

After breakfast, my cell door clanked open automatically. "Parker, G-North—grab your linens and come out here."

I hurriedly grabbed the blankets and sheets and my Bible, following the keeper through the lockups in a stunned daze.

Am I getting released? Or are they simply playing a big game with me, just to see how I will react? Can't let them know how I feel . . . ."

Reaching the end of the walkway, the guard mumbled, "I don't know how it happened, but you're gettin' out."

Joyfully, I remembered "Patience, son . . . soon." Still, it was hard to believe that the judge had signed our release. *Any second now, they'll tell me I have to go back—that the paper work is wrong, or that the judge changed his mind.* With every single step; down the cell-block corridor, down the stairs, through the room where I had picked up my bedding upon entrance to the facility, upon shedding the orange jail coveralls, showering and donning my crumpled street clothes; these thoughts plagued me.

The guard led me to another holding cell. "You'll have to wait in there until your paper work's done, Parker."

Just hurry up, I murmured. Turning to the right, I sat apprehensively on a steel bench along the wall. I wasn't alone. The bank robber I had met in the Barstow jail sat across from me. *Oh, no! What if he heard why I'm here and wants to start a fight? That could keep me from being released. Oh, Lord, don't let anything go wrong now. Please.*

"Oh, are you being freed, too?" I asked, trying to be friendly.

"Naw. Just being extradited to Arizona."

We lapsed into silence until two FBI agents entered and escorted the man out. It seemed like forever before a deputy came for me.

"Okay, Parker, let's go," he beckoned through the open door. I followed him to a counter where I was given the envelope with my personal effects.

"Is my wife being released also?"

"It'll be a few minutes. You'll have to wait in the lobby."

Soon I was passing through a door into freedom. Sitting on a bench in the lobby, I stared through the large glass doors that stood between me and the outside. When Lucky emerged from the women's facility, she looked dazed. We met halfway across the room and embraced with tears of joy trickling down our faces, hugging each other tightly.

Once outside, we walked briskly down the steps and away from the building that had been our hell for the past week. Suddenly, freedom became something we could touch. Being able to see the sky and know that it was daytime, feeling the air on our faces, watching the trees wave gently in the breeze, knowing that we could again hug our children and be with them—one cannot imagine the wonder of these blessings after such a week of confinement.

With the traffic whizzing by us, I suddenly realized that we had no transportation back to Barstow. Our first thought had been to get as far from the jail as possible. I knew we had enough money for bus fare.

Lucky grabbed my arm and pointed to a yellow station wagon passing slowly by. "Look, Larry. That's my lawyer. He's waving at us."

As the driver maneuvered his car around, Lucky told me how they had met. "That's Leroy Simmons. I met him last Saturday when he came to tell me that the court had appointed him. He's a private attorney in Barstow."

Lee pulled the car up next to us, rolled down his window and called, "Hi there—I heard you were being released just a few minutes ago and wanted to catch you before you left. Good timing, eh?"

Lucky grinned in agreement. I just stood there, wondering what to say to this stranger.

"Get in. I'm Lee Simmons," the man greeted me, extending his hand as we slipped into the front seat.

"Oh," I smiled weakly.

"Have you heard of me?"

"No, I'm sorry, I haven't."

Lee grinned, "Do you folks have a ride home to Barstow?"

We shook our heads.

"Well, then let's drive home together. I live in Barstow, too."

Heading toward the business district of San Bernardino, Lee asked, "You folks want a cold drink? I'm going to stop and get one."

"Yes, that'd be fine," we chorused.

On our way to Barstow, we became better acquainted with Lucky's attorney, discussing our concern for the children. We had been told that they would be released that day into the custody of my brother and sister-in-law. We could visit but not take them home to live.

A religious man, Lee asked us about our understanding of faith. His church also believed in anointing the sick with oil and in the laying on of hands for healing, he commented, perhaps trying to make us feel more at ease.

As we rode through Cajon Pass, out of the smoggy air of the San Bernardino basin and into the relatively unpolluted high desert, I let my mind wander—unfocusing and focusing on the rock formations at the bottom of the pass. I visualized turn-of-the-century outlaws riding about on their horses, regaled in western garb, recalling those colorful moments of the Old West. I chuckled at my thoughts as we glided along, six inches above the ribbon of highway that snaked through the pass, relaxing in the air-conditioned comfort of Lee's car. I was free, as free as those cowboys who roamed the ranges of yesteryear. Well, maybe not *as* free. We still had those charges hanging over our heads.

Pulling into our driveway, Lee advised us to get some rest and call his office in a couple of days for an appointment.

"You can explain everything that happened at that time," he smiled.

A few minutes later we were on our way to Tony's and Carol's to see the children.

"You know that Bible I picked up from the light stand the day of our arrest?" Lucky asked.

"It's Wesley's," I commented.

"Uh huh. I had it all the time we were in jail. I read mostly through the Psalms, but one day I was thumbing through the New Testament and came across a verse that Wesley himself had bracketed out. In 1 Thessalonians 5:18 it says, "In everything give thanks: for this is the will of God in Christ Jesus concerning you." When I read it, I just broke into tears because it was like Wess was telling me that," she cried. "It was hard to accept, but the Lord used that to help me."

Lucky paused for a few moments, trying to retain her composure. Finally, she spoke, looking up into my face with tear-filled eyes. "You know, that one thing made me think a lot about Wess, and . . . about whether we, ah, made a mistake.

"I mean, I was wondering if we had done something wrong, misinterpreted or something. I told the Lord that I was sorry if I had done anything wrong by withholding Wesley's insulin . . . just to be on the safe side. Larry . . . what if the Lord doesn't intend . . . to bring him back?"

I jerked to face her, my eyes burning like hot coals. "Don't you think that!" I hissed. "We just *can't* think that. Wesley must rise. God's Word promised . . . even if he didn't come back on the fourth day like I expected."

The voice I was hearing sounded firm, resolute. It was unlike what was going on inside my mind: A wave of doubt pouring on the dying embers of hope for Wesley's return, the last flicker of faith being quenched in the flood waters of fear. I did not want to face the possibility that we could have been mistaken.

9

"Not *Everything* You Did Was Right"

I was lying on my back, the light outside the cell shining through the barred door casting long, thin shadows across my face. I stared through the bars to the fog outside. Softly chilling, it rolled and swirled, yet never entered my cell. I felt dead, like Wesley lying in the cold ground back in Barstow. The thought of my young son brought tears, which finally trickled down my face, leaving glistening tracks. Suddenly, a typically loud "slam" sat me upright in the bunk . . .

. . . and I was looking straight out my bedroom window; the desert sunshine was streaming through. *Dream*, I sighed, wiping my damp cheeks with a sheet. *Just a dream.*

The early morning sun had warmed the bedroom to a comfortable temperature. My half-awake ears heard another "slam," and I bolted out of the bed. Lucky was up. From the noises passing through the bedroom wall, it was evident where she was.

"Larry, you up?" she called.

"Yeah." I hobbled to the chair upon which I had thrown my clothes the night before and began to dress. On my way out, I picked up my watch from the nightstand. *Eight o'clock.*

To my surprise, Mardi Clay and another friend were sitting in the living room, reading their Bibles. When I entered, they looked up, smiled and greeted me in unison.

"Hi, Larry."

Embarrassed that I wasn't dressed for company, I retreated hastily back through the hall into the bedroom and slipped on a shirt, socks and shoes.

"Lucky! Why didn't you tell me we had company?" My words were louder than she could bear.

"Shhh," she warned menacingly. "I didn't know you were out of bed."

"Okay, okay—but what are *they* doing out there?"

"They came over just a few minutes ago to give us a little moral support. Today's our preliminary hearing, don't forget."

I was calmer now. "Yeah, I know. You're right . . . it's great that they're here."

After about an hour of just talking and prayer, we sat quietly, reading our Bibles. Lucky had gone to the bedroom to be alone and pray. My eyes hungrily searched the Psalms for solace. Suddenly, several verses in Psalm 109 seemed to stand out. Startled, I read them again, and again:

> My knees are weak through fasting; and my flesh faileth of fatness.
>
> I became also a reproach unto them: when they looked upon me they shook their heads.
>
> Help me, O Lord my God: O save me according to Thy mercy: That they may know that this is Thy hand; that thou, Lord, hast done it.
>
> Let them curse, but bless thou: when they arise, let them be ashamed; but let thy servant rejoice. Let mine adversaries be clothed with

shame, and let them cover themselves with
their own confusion, as with a mantle.

I will greatly praise the Lord with my
mouth; yea, I will praise him among the
multitude.

For he shall stand at the right hand of the
poor, to save him from those that condemn his
soul.

I lifted my head from reading these verses, amazed
at how they so accurately spoke to our situation. Not
only had we been fasting, we had become a reproach
to the citizens of Barstow. Many times since our release
from jail, neighbors had called us murderers and child
killers. Eggs had been thrown at our house, and we
had received anonymous threats in the mail and over
the phone. In town Lucky would be met with sneers
and dirty looks. One day on her way home, she had
stopped at a stop sign. When the motorist who had the
right of way recognized Lucky in passing, he made a
hateful face and stuck out his tongue. We had been
continually seeking God in prayer for a way to show
the public, the courts, and our church that we only
had done what we thought was in God's will.

Still, I was puzzled over the words of the Psalm: ". . .
Let them be ashamed . . . Let mine adversaries be
clothed with shame . . . ." I rose from my seat with the
open Bible and walked slowly to the bedroom to see
Lucky kneeling at the side of our bed, fretting.

"Honey, I just read something, right here in the
Psalms that I feel is a message from the Lord for us today," I spoke almost apologetically for disturbing her
fretful prayers. Her face was pinched in fright when I
finished reading.

"Well, that sounds kind of tough. I don't want to hurt anyone—I don't want vengeance, or anyone to be ashamed. I just want them to leave us alone," she objected, staring straight ahead at the wall.

"I don't quite understand it either, but I definitely feel it's from the Lord. We'll have to wait and see . . . ."

Our hearing was scheduled for eleven o'clock. As we drove through the pleasant Barstow morning to the municipal courthouse, I pondered the meaning of those puzzling verses. We parked at the corner near the building, hoping to avoid the newsmedia and television cameras. As we approached the flat, tan-colored building, the onslaught of questions by the press began: "Do you still believe Wesley's going to rise?" "How do you feel about this hearing?" Remembering our lawyers' stern warning, we pushed past the reporters without a word.

Newsmen and curious spectators were jammed into the busy courtroom; some were standing. We found a couple of seats on the left side of the aisle. It was a small room, painted yellow with dark wooden rails and furnishings. As I surveyed the room for our attorneys, a side door opened, and Lee Simmons strode in. Greeting us with a smile, he leaned over to whisper, "Larry . . . Lucky . . . uh, why don't you follow me. I have a place where you can be alone, away from the stares of these people."

I recognized the door through which he led us. It opened into the deliberation room for a jury, ironically the same one in which I had sat a few years before as the foreman of the jury.

"You just sit tight while I check to see when your case will be called," he instructed. Lucky and I sat at the table in the center of the room, opened our Bibles and began to read. The passage in Psalm 109 still struck a strong chord of hope in my heart.

Suddenly, the door burst open and Lee rushed in, quickly closing it behind him. His face carried a look of astonishment. "I just can't believe it!" he blurted. "I really don't believe this has happened."

Lucky and I glanced at each other in surprise and suspense. Had the judge dismissed our case? Lee's eyes narrowed as his voice lowered to a stage whisper. "Promise not to repeat this? At least not to the reporters outside?"

We nodded. *"What*, Lee? Tell us what happened!"

"Right now, this moment, in another room off to the side of the courtroom, there are several deputies physically restraining the deputy D.A. from entering the court."

"Why?" I asked impatiently.

Lee looked me in the eye and exclaimed, "He's drunk on his feet! It's eleven o'clock in the morning, and the prosecutor is loaded to the gills. There's no way he can present evidence to the judge to show that you should be held over for trial. No way!"

I looked down at my Bible, still opened to Psalm 109, put my hands on the book and pushed it toward the attorney, turning it so he could read.

"Read this, Lee. Verse twenty-nine. The Lord is using that passage to tell us everything will be all right. When I read it this morning, the meaning was unclear. But I understand it now."

Lee picked up the Bible and began to read: "Let mine adversaries be clothed with shame, and let them cover themselves with their own confusion, as with a mantle." He looked up, smiled weakly, and shrugged skeptically.

The prosecutor was indeed our "adversary." Surely in his drunkenness he was covered with his "own confusion, as with a mantle." And when he sobered, he would be "clothed with shame." I grinned, not at our adversary's misfortune, but at the fulfillment of that Bible verse. Now I felt that God had not abandoned us.

Later we learned the details behind the prosecutor's condition. In a cocktail lounge the night before, he had stood and shook his fist, cursing furiously, "I'm going to get those Parkers tomorrow." It made me remember the verse, "Let them curse . . . when they arise, let them be ashamed; but let thy servant rejoice." Eventually the man lost his job.

Learning of the deputy district attorney's drunkenness, the judge postponed our hearing to the following week. He banged his gavel loudly to adjourn the court, and we were led by Lee through the back door, down a brightly-lit hallway, and out the rear exit to avoid the reporters. Feeling a sense of triumph over the relentless bloodhounds of the press, we descended the hill and strode around the block toward our car. A lone man stood glaring down at us, expressing once again the hatred of the town.

We drove past the courthouse, amused that the reporters and T.V. cameramen were still outside, waiting for us to come out.

"How 'bout some lunch?" I asked, turning the corner.

"Take me home, and I'll fix you a good one . . . ."

We had attended our church in Barstow the Sunday after our releases from jail, but felt unwelcome. Some of the people had turned their backs to us; others had instructed their children not to play with ours. A few had extended their sympathy, but most just stood and stared. In view of this we had decided to drive the thirty miles into Victorville to visit another church of our denomination.

That congregation extended a gracious welcome. Many of the people didn't know we were "the Parkers from Barstow," of course. We decided early in the first service that we would worship here—at least until time healed the injury so keenly felt in Barstow.

Now as we drove toward that church, I was looking forward to the service. Dick Mills, an evangelist who had a unique ministry of quoting Bible verses to people who had need for a special "word from the Lord," would be speaking. We had never seen this man's ministry in action, and were curious. My hope that he could help us today was strong, for I desperately needed guidance for the days ahead.

Lucky and I pulled into the parking lot about fifteen minutes early, parked, and quickly walked to the sanctuary to find good seats. The auditorium was practically full, and we were fortunate to find two seats near the rear.

The service opened with a few hymns, and soon we were ready, emotionally and spiritually, for whatever the Lord had for us. Finally it was time for Mills to speak.

"I feel that the Lord would have me minister to a specific group of people today . . ." he began, his voice forceful, authoritative. He stood behind the pulpit, hands clasping firmly to its side. He is a powerfully built man, full of energy and enthusiasm for the Word of God. ". . . people involved in professional law enforcement. I have a special burden on my heart at this time for you. If you are a police officer, a deputy sheriff, or in any way connected with this line of work, please come to the front. I want to minister the Word to you."

I was surprised at the number of people who went forward. As they lined up at the altar, he took each one by the hand, looked them straight in the eye, and began to quote verses from the Old and New Testaments aimed at their individual needs. His wife wrote the references on a small pad and handed the slip of paper to each person as he returned to his seat.

I was disappointed that Lucky and I would not be helped that morning. We would return that evening, when there usually weren't so many people. Perhaps then the evangelist would minister to us.

While the children and I ate our noon meal, Lucky secluded herself in our bedroom to pray. Secretly since our conversation on the way to Tony's and Carol's the day we were released from jail, she had wrestled with the thought, *Was what we did wrong?*

I refused to listen to such an idea, for how was I to keep my faith for Wesley's imminent resurrection if Lucky continued to express doubt? Of course we were right! We were just following the Lord's leading at the time . . . weren't we?

Now as she agonized in prayer, Lucky desperately called on God to reveal the truth to us. "If You're not going to bring Wess back," she wept, "let me know: Did we do anything wrong? We honestly believed we were doing right, Lord. But the results keep saying we were wrong."

That night we sat in the middle pews of the church. To my dismay there were more people. As Mills stepped to the platform, his boundless energy burst through every pore. He immediately went to work, selecting people in the first few rows of pews for his special "words from the Lord." Again he quoted Bible verses as the people stood before him; again his smiling wife handed the reference to them as he finished and went on to the next person. Lucky sighed forlornly when Mills finished and headed for the pulpit to give his sermon. I stared at him, wondering, *Perhaps the Lord will use this man to help us after the service.*

Suddenly, Mills stopped speaking in mid-sentence and scanned the auditorium. "Uh, there's a couple here tonight to whom the Lord wants me to minister before I begin." He paused for a moment as though waiting to receive instructions from God. "They're surrounded and pressed in on every side . . . ."

He began to relate, in a general way, our circumstances; everything he said seemed to point at us and shout, "That's you!"

"The Lord wants to minister to you," he concluded. "If you're here, and believe that I'm talking about you, stand up."

We needed no coaxing. As we shot up out of our seats, the eyes of everyone riveted on us.

"I don't know who you are, or even if you're the couple God's talking about," he began hesitantly, "but if you are, this is God's word for you tonight. I have a definite impression that what you are going through is not just affecting you, but many others also . . . ."

He closed his eyes in concentration, then opened them quickly and continued to speak, rapidly now. I took Lucky's hand and felt her tension and uneasiness cut loose and waft away.

"Exodus 14:13 and 14 says, 'Fear ye not, stand still,

and see the salvation of the Lord, which he will show to you today: for the Egyptians whom ye have seen today, ye shall see them again no more forever. The Lord shall fight for you, and ye shall hold your peace.' "

It had been about three weeks since our release from jail. I thought of our guards as the Egyptians when I pictured the context of those verses and took them to mean that we wouldn't be living behind bars.

He continued, "Deuteronomy 33:27 and 29 says, 'The eternal God is thy refuge, and underneath are the everlasting arms: and He shall thrust out the enemy from before thee; and shall say, Destroy them. Happy art thou, O Israel: who is like unto thee, O people saved by the Lord, the shield of thy help, and who is thy sword of thy excellency and thine enemies shall be found liars unto thee; and thou shalt tread upon their high places.'

". . . . Isaiah 41:11 and 12 says, 'Behold all they that were incensed against thee shall be ashamed and confounded: they shall be as nothing; and they that strive with thee shall perish. Thou shalt seek them, and shalt not find them, even them that contend with thee: they that war against thee shall be as nothing, and as a thing of nought,' " Mills quoted.

I recalled our canceled preliminary hearing and thought of the shame the prosecutor must have felt when he sobered. I remembered grimly the many times we had been called murderers and child killers, the times we had cleaned up broken eggs. These people would be confounded—but by what? My heart thumped in anticipation. It would have to be something *big*. Like Wesley's resurrection?

Dick Mills shook his head slowly, and then looking up abruptly, stared us straight in the eyes.

"There *is* one more thing." A puzzled look crossed his face. "The Lord wants you to know that not *everything* you did was right."

His voice was still firm, but not as dynamic as it had been during his recitation of the Bible. Instead, it was breathed upon us like a pleasant, warm, humid breeze. It seemed that the Lord was gently probing my heart, pushing and pulling at the same time.

I heard Lucky whisper, "Oh, Lord, if not *everything* we did was right, then something *was* wrong."

As we sat down, Betty Mills walked from the front and handed Lucky the slip of paper upon which she had written the references. Lucky folded it and slipped it into her Bible.

Mills began to preach, but I could hear nothing except those last words: "Not everything you did was right." I was determined to speak with this evangelist after the meeting. Lucky and I walked up to the altar afterward and waited for an opportunity to talk with him. He finally finished praying for those who had responded to his call, and I stepped forward.

"Brother Mills, do you know who we are?"

"Well . . . no," he hesitated.

"We're the Parkers . . ." I paused to see if he recognized our name. ". . . the people whose son died of diabetes."

Suddenly, he remembered. "Oh . . . yes," he scowled. "I read about that in the newspaper."

"Brother Mills, I'm really concerned about what was said tonight. Can you tell us just how we were wrong?"

"Is there some place we can go to get away from the people?" he hesitated.

I asked an usher nearby, who told us of a hallway behind the platform. We could find privacy there.

Alone with us, Mills seemed tense, telling us of his feelings of hostility when he read of our ordeal.

"It was wrong for you to force this upon your son," he counseled curtly.

"But we didn't force *anything* upon Wesley. When his urine test showed he needed insulin, Wess prepared his injection as usual, but I told him the symptoms were just a lie of Satan, and he was healed—Wess was thrilled. But if he'd asked for the insulin during his suffering, we would have given it immediately," I defended.

He looked confused and was silent for a moment. "Well . . . you can't always believe everything you read in the papers," he apologized. His attitude changed suddenly into one of compassion. He smiled and took us by the hands.

"God, right now, is flooding me with love for you. And I feel like He wants you to know that He loves you very much. The Lord is going to bring you into new relationships, and give you new friends as the result of Wesley's death."

Lucky and I left the church that night relieved and confident that God truly did care for us and had the circumstances of our lives under control. My resistance had subsided to the fact that we were in error—in at least one aspect of our actions. But what? Perhaps it was our mistake that was even now preventing his resurrection. Somehow, we needed to correct whatever we had done so Wess could still be raised from the dead.

10

Held to Answer in "Faith" Death

Snapping off the rubber band that held the newspaper in a folded position, I opened it to expose the front page. A small headline at the bottom caught my eye:

Parkers held
to answer in
'faith' death

I winced at the title and sat down in a chair next to our table lamp to read:

"BARSTOW—Lawrence and Alice Parker were held to answer criminal charges yesterday in the 'faith healing' death of their 11-year-old diabetic son, Wesley.

"Judge Ted L. DeBord of the Barstow Municipal Court District ordered the Parkers to appear at 9 a.m. Oct. 9 in Superior Court, San Bernardino, to have a date set for their trial. DeBord's ruling followed a preliminary hearing on charges of manslaughter and child abuse against the Parkers.

"The Parkers are accused of withholding the insulin treatment for their son's diabetes from Aug. 19 to Aug.

22, when the boy died. The Parkers previously said they believed their son had been healed by a visiting minister at their church Aug. 19 and Wesley would be resurrected."

My face burned as I read that last sentence. Why didn't the reporter write about the agony we went through? Why did he just lump it all together in one sentence without attempting to explain how we arrived at our conclusions?

"Following arguments by Dept. Dist. Atty. Don Feld and defense attorneys LeRoy Simmons and Samuel Weiss, the judge said 'It's not often you have the motive offered in defense—it's usually part of the prosecution.'

"Simmons had argued that the state Welfare Code provides that parents are allowed to seek 'other remedial care' besides medical attention in the treatment of their children. He said the law allows for the healing by faith.

" 'The use of faith is a well-recognized method of remedial care,' he said. 'Because it failed, (this) does not render of any less value the ability to use it.'

"Feld said the Parkers should be held to answer the charges because precedents in law have ruled out religious belief as a defense in such cases. 'If a religion allowed human sacrifice,' he asked, 'would such practices be allowed to continue?' "

I had been offended at that statement. How could he equate what we did to human sacrifice? Our attorney's defense was based upon his premise that the laws on healing by faith did apply. The context in which these laws were found, however, applied only to the beliefs of Christian Science. Since our denomination did not hold such tenets, the judge discounted Lee's argument.

We had hoped that the case would be dismissed, but Mr. Feld presented enough evidence to bring us to trial. Lucky and I were disappointed that no witnesses were called on our behalf, but our counselors did not want to reveal their strategy for defense. The prosecutor *did* present witnesses, our friends, and their testimony was convincing.

We were accused of *wanting* to believe that Wess was healed, even though the symptoms were otherwise. "It was clear he was ill," Feld had said. "God was talking to them, but they didn't listen. They did not want to listen." I had felt such anger at the prosecutor for calling on friends to testify. Neither did I appreciate his assumptions as to how Wesley's death occurred.

I put the paper down on my lap and stared straight ahead, wondering how this case would develop. Outside, the cold fingers of the desert dawn were just beginning to tug at the skirts of night. Inside, this beautiful sight was wasted on a hollow shell of a man who only strove for normalcy in his life.

My mind drifted back to the comments made by Mardi Clay to Lucky a day or two after our meeting with Dick Mills . . . and the stubborn resistance I had expressed as Lucky related the incident.

Mardi had visited a minister in Anaheim, California, whose wife had been healed of diabetes, hoping he would have some insight into what went wrong in our case. We were in error, the preacher had explained, by applying faith unscripturally. God cannot honor His Word when it is misused. We had tied His hands by trying to force Him into healing Wesley, not realizing the difference between proving and tempting God.

The minister gave the illustration of Jesus going to the pinnacle of the temple in Jerusalem, where the devil had tempted Him to prove God. "If thou be the Son of God, cast thyself down," Satan had sneered, "for it is written, 'He shall give his angels charge concerning thee: and in their hands they shall bear thee up' . . ." Jesus' response had been, "Thou shall not *tempt* the Lord thy God."[1] He believed that we had acted presumptuously in trying to prove God and our faith, when all the while we were tempting the Lord instead. Our sin of withholding Wesley's insulin had hindered his healing, for God cannot answer "faith" that is rooted in presumption.

Perhaps Mr. Feld's observation was accurate: God was talking to us, but we weren't listening. Still, the idea of someone telling us that we did wrong grated me. My mind resented the preacher's evaluation and my mind stumbled at Dick Mill's words, but my heart had begun its quest for the truth.

During the months between the preliminary hearing and our trial, which began on May 22, 1974, God continually comforted us and met our needs. Our children were returned to our custody, and other miracles occurred. We received calls and letters of support from around the country, some encouraging me to hold on for Wesley's resurrection, others containing cash donations. These helped us through the rough times when my unemployment benefits stopped. We had been liv-

1.Matt. 4:5-7. See also *From the Pinnacle of the Temple* by Dr. Charles Farah Jr., Logos (Plainfield, NJ, nd).

ing by faith from day to day like this for several weeks when my old job as an electronics technician at NASA's Goldstone Satellite Tracking Station near Barstow was restored.

Back to work and my family life renewed, I continued to search for the basis of our error. Lucky, meanwhile, was wrestling with her own agony: "Lord, I'm so tired of struggling. I know we did wrong, but is Wesley coming back?" Each time she would receive a strong inward impression, as though the Lord were answering, "Don't look back. Just look to Me—not to circumstances or to people. Stay in My Word."

Finally in December before the year of our trial, Lucky settled the matter in her heart. She would not expect Wess to come back. But in my quest for the truth, I still searched for the key to Wesley's resurrection, unable emotionally to let my son go.

Our understanding of the error developed slowly, perhaps beginning to dawn the Sunday night in Victorville when another evangelist spoke on faith and healing.

As his message unfolded, we were horrified. He was telling the people to take verses from the Bible and claim them for personal use. *God, that's what we did,* I reasoned. *If this is the right way to do things, where did we go wrong?*

"Now don't misunderstand what I'm saying," the speaker suddenly cautioned sarcastically, unaware we were in the audience. "Don't act like your neighbors over in Barstow who didn't give their child insulin. They were definitely wrong."

Our badly-healing wounds were ripped open again by this man's reckless speech. I wanted desperately to jump up and yell, "Hey, mister! We're the Parkers. We did exactly what you're telling everyone here to do. Why don't you tell us what we did wrong?"

After the service, the pianist handed me a note that was comforting. It read:

> . . . Please forgive all the Christian brothers and sisters who may seem critical. They haven't been through as much as you have. The Lord must know you are strong enough to rise above it. We're glad to have you fellowshiping with us.

I was obviously troubled as we drove homeward across the star-lit desert. "That preacher burned me up!" I grumbled angrily. "The thing he was talking about tonight—positive confession, or whatever you call it—that's what we did. We took the Word, confessed it, stood upon it, claimed it, and held God responsible to fulfill it. But I'm beginning to believe there's something more to it. Maybe we need specific direction from God before we can do this."

Lucky didn't respond. She sat silently, letting the tears flow in the dusk. Later, Lucky told me how she and Mardi had been listening to some tapes from a minister in the midwest who says the Holy Spirit is gentle, not in a hurry. He doesn't pressure us. He gives us time to pray and consider things.

"I never felt that when we prayed for Wess," she acknowledged. "This minister says that pressure, hurrying, confusion is the enemy's way—not God's."

"Are you saying we were deceived by Satan?" I spat impatiently.

"We were mistaken, Larry. We just didn't know what we were doing. The Old Testament says, 'My people perish for lack of knowledge.' Maybe our son perished because of our lack of knowledge." Lucky began to cry.

Could this have been our error? Believing a lie of the devil? Had God chosen another way, another time to heal Wess? What was preventing Wesley from returning? Or would he come back at all?

"God, strengthen my faith . . . ." I was at work on the swing shift, taking advantage of a lull in our satellite tracking to stroll around the station grounds. The slowly circling dish-like white antenna was brightly illuminated against the starry sky. My mind was struggling to reason out the series of spiritual events that had filled my life recently.

In one week we would be standing trial, pleading "not guilty" to charges that accused us of doing wrong. I smiled at the irony. We had rejected our lawyers' advice to plea bargain. We wanted to be found innocent of all charges—which pleased our lawyers. Lee believed that our case could be carried to the Supreme Court and probably would rewrite the law in regards to the use of faith healing. "It's bigger than the Scope's monkey trial . . . ." he would say. (This case concerned freedom to teach the theory of evolution in the schools.)

Yet the trial was not the source of my apprehension now. I took a long breath and exhaled slowly, my eyes gazing at the massive canopy of stars, then stretched and groaned to squeeze the tiredness from my muscles. Again my mind pleaded with God for an increase of faith. As I sent small pebbles skipping across the sand into the wild, low-growing mesquite, my thoughts returned to the conversation Lucky and I had about some Bible "promises."

"How can those verses on prosperity be for everyone?" she had wondered. "If that's the case, why are so many Christians poor? And if the Bible promises healing, why isn't everyone healed?"

We had always been taught that such failures came because one didn't "believe enough." If you believed enough, you would act like you had received it, and the answer would come; "launching out into the deep," where you couldn't touch bottom was the kind of faith that God honored.

Perhaps one cannot arbitrarily take a verse from the Bible and say, "I'm going to stand on it." But there was no doubt in our minds that the Bible is for everyone, and that anyone *could* claim its promises. Still, a balance existed somewhere. Perhaps these promises had to be *given*, inspired by the Holy Spirit to a person for a specific need. This was the case with the verses given to us by Dick Mills, and with the verses quickened to me on the day our first preliminary hearing that was canceled when our adversary was "clothed with shame."

With the trial so near, Jeremiah 39:17 and 18 had become a great comfort to Lucky. "I will deliver thee in that day, saith the Lord: and thou shalt not be given into the hand of the men of whom thou art afraid. For I will surely deliver thee . . . because thou hast put thy trust in me, saith the Lord."

In these days we were being *given* the promises of God.

I felt tense walking around the station, my mind blocking out the beautiful desert night as I pondered these issues. Still on my break, I returned to my post, opened my Bible to the small concordance in the back, and began looking up verses on faith. 1 Corinthians 13:13 stood out from the rest. "And now abideth faith, hope, love, these three; but the greatest of these is *love.*"

That one word—*love*—seemed to leap from the page. I tried futilely to get my mind back on faith, but the locomotive in my brain had rumbled onto a new track. In those startling moments the Lord had begun to illuminate the path that would lead me to the greatest discovery of my life.

11

"Faith Rests"

With the words ". . . the greatest of these is love . . ." still pounding in my mind, I returned mentally to the present and once more focused on the courtroom drama before me.

On this second day of our trial, that word "love" was again driven to my heart. The words of Cindy Wilson had stunned the prosecutor who had hoped to use her testimony to score a major point for his case.

"Now, Mrs. Wilson, other than an occasional drink of water and some prayer, was there anything else that was given to Wesley while you were there?"

"Love," she had responded.

Now, as Cindy was further questioned, the gravity of our situation focused sharply on an even more painful aspect of our dilemma. Prosecutor Tom Frazier haughtily stepped closer to the witness stand and looked Cindy straight in the eye.

"You made an interesting statement on cross examination by Mr. Russler," he smiled wryly. "You said, 'If it is God.' "

Frazier raised his eyebrows at Cindy, implying that he expected her to answer.

"Yes," she said, squirming in her seat.

"Indicating that possibly there may be . . . ."

"I am going to object to Counsel's speech-making, Your Honor," Lee Simmons interrupted. "I think that's leading, suggestive to the witness."

Judge Williams thoughtfully looked down to the deputy district attorney. "I think the question could be better phrased." Turning slightly to Cindy, he asked, "What did you mean by that?"

Looking up to the judge, she swallowed hard. "By 'if it is God?' "

"Yes."

Cindy turned to face the court, then dropped her eyes to avoid Frazier's steady stare. "Well, if you believe in God, you have to believe in the devil, too . . . ." My stomach soured at the rest of her statement, realizing that it was true. ". . . and he has power, too. He can deceive you."

Frazier smiled kindly, "Do you think it is possible for the devil to deceive people from time to time?"

"Yes."

"And that some things that people might believe are from God may actually be from the devil?"

"Yes."

Frazier turned abruptly to the judge and nodded sneeringly, "I have nothing further." He strode confidently to the Counselors' table and sat down.

"No further questions, Your Honor," our lawyers intoned.

The judge nodded to Cindy. "Thank you. You may step down."

My thoughts were haunted by her statement on deception as other witnesses took the stand: *Were Lucky and I deceived?*

On our way home that evening, I was more receptive to Lucky's reflections on our situation.

"Larry," she began hesitantly, "we didn't show Wesley as much love as we could have. When I read my Bible, words like 'love never fails' and 'faith working through love' keep popping out at me."

Crossing the Mojave River, my eyes remained glued to the upward sweep of the highway. Encouraged by my silence, she began to speak more quickly.

"I feel pain when I see the word 'love.' I'm beginning to see that God doesn't let someone suffer to give him healing . . . what we did wasn't God's way . . . His love never fails. It was less than loving when we allowed Wess to suffer."

"I don't know, honey," I sighed after a long silence. "I just don't know . . . ."

We finally drove into the Barstow city limits, exhausted from our day of trial and the long drive to and from San Bernardino. Our daily schedule had been hectic for the past two weeks of jury selection and the first two days of trial: We'd get up early to take the children to a friend's house, who would send them off to school, then we'd drive to San Bernardino for the trial, back to Barstow, pick up the kids, come home, eat dinner, and collapse into bed.

"This commute is killing us," I muttered driving up to our friend's house. We rounded up the kids into the car and minutes later pulled into our driveway—a car filled with grouchy grownups and cranky children. We were hardly prepared for what awaited us! The plumbing had backed up and flooded the floors. Frustrated, we grabbed a mop and towels and began cleaning up the mess.

Under the duress of mopping floors, life seemed overwhelming. Not only was our schedule exhausting,

but our old car was not in shape for the long daily
roundtrips, and the price of gas would soon be more
than fifty cents a gallon!

In desperation we called my mother in Maryland,
asking her to come out and stay with the children. We
would live with friends in San Bernardino during the
week and come home weekends.

While we were in jail, Lucky and I had been visited
by two people—Larry Montoya and Lois Brown—who
lived in San Bernardino. They had told us to contact
them if we needed any help. The next day when we
were in the big city for the trial, we called Lois and
Larry. Both gladly opened their homes. Dick Mills had
told us that new friends and relationships would come
out of our crisis. Lois, Larry and his wife, Dorothy,
were fulfilling that prediction.

The third day of the trial seemed even more painful.
Frazier called as the prosecution's witness the man who
had performed the autopsy on Wesley—Dr. Chester
Holt. The prosecutor's probing questions made his
description of Wesley's autopsy gruesome. Visions of
our child being picked apart, piece by piece, made me
physically ill.

At one point in Dr. Holt's testimony, the prosecutor
tried to picture Lucky and me as abusive and cruel.
Citing minor bruises on Wesley's leg, Frazier attempted to prove that we constantly beat our child and
that our withholding Wesley's insulin was not an
isolated case of abuse. Although Dr. Holt stifled
Frazier's line of questioning—saying that for a boy of
eleven, minor bruises on the legs were normal, if not
customary—the prosecutor had driven home another
arrow.

As the trial dragged on for weeks, I viewed it as a

small war, with each side furiously battling the other. The lawyers cleverly drew out statements from many of our friends that were used for and against us. One of these was Pastor Gary Nash.

Through their barrage of questions, the lawyers unveiled our denomination's stand on such things as faith, the use of medicine, divine healing and, painfully, the church's stand on the Parkers.

"Okay, Reverend Nash . . . . You knew Wesley Parker?" Bill Russler began.

"Yes."

"Was he an intelligent boy?"

"I would say so."

"You prayed with him?"

"Yes."

"To your observation, were the Parkers loving and affectionate parents?"

"Yes."

"During the time that you were at the Parker household on Wednesday, August the twenty-second, nineteen seventy-three, did you have any doubt that the Parkers were sincere?"

"No, I think they were sincere in what they were doing at that time."

"Thank you," my attorney concluded, stepping back from the stand. "I have no further questions."

Frazier stood and waved a piece of paper. "Your Honor, at this time we would move that People's Exhibit Number Twelve be introduced as evidence."

Still standing near the witness stand, Russler interrupted. "Is that Reverend Nash's letter of August twenty-fourth, nineteen seventy-three?"

"Yes."

"I have no objection." Russler walked back to the Counselors' table.

"To speed it up," Judge Williams injected, "I will let you read the letter to the jury at this time. They can examine it later."

The prosecutor began to read Pastor Nash's response to our actions regarding Wesley. Still on the witness stand, he began to weep, turning his head away from the jury so they would not see. My eyes began to mist also as I heard the harsh words that he had written; words, I was sure, that were difficult, even painful, for him to write.

"Dear church member," Frazier read dramatically. "As pastor, I was opposed to the methods used by those praying for the healing of Wesley Parker. I say with full assurance in my heart that it was not of God and voiced my opinion of this to Larry Parker prior to the death of Wesley. There was a witness present who also endeavored to advise Larry Parker. Our advice was rejected.

"Let me also make clear that I believe God can do anything He so desires in healing the sick and raising the dead. But there is no reason for God to raise Wesley Parker from the dead, and (to) any sincere people in our church who have asked me personally, I have expressed this very strongly . . . .

"I do not believe that Wesley Parker was demon possessed, neither do I believe any Christian can be demon possessed. The word 'Christian' means Christlikeness. No Christlike person would have the devil dwelling in him. It would be a divided house . . . .

"I believe in the gifts of the Spirit in operation, but God does not have to permit a small child to go through suffering and torment, die and be resurrected;

all of this was done at Calvary. If those who believed
Wesley Parker's sickness was demon possession, they
would also believe he died demon possessed. If he died
demon possessed, he would go to the place of the abode
of wicked spirits. No one has ever been resurrected
from Hell.

"Those who have been swallowed up in all of this
confusion over the last couple of months have fulfilled
Scripture, which states that in the last days there
would be doctrines of devils, and sincere people would
be deceived.

"Several people have been implicated into this matter, which will in the very near future arise to a very
serious situation. It will draw the full attention of not
only the City of Barstow, but the county, state, and
perhaps even the nation. I intend to do everything in a
Christian manner, and my full intent is to protect the
Lord's name . . . the local church and, above all, every
sincere member of the body of Christ.

"For some reason, God has permitted an innocent
child to suffer and die. But God never makes mistakes.
The work of God which has begun here in Barstow
shall go forward, and at this time your church needs
your full support in every way. I believe Wesley has
gone to be with the Lord. Let's not let his death to have
been in vain, but from it God's work shall be
strengthened and the kingdom of God enlarged . . . .

"There will be a special prayer meeting at nine every
morning next week at the church. For this reason I am
personally opposed to any prayer meetings taking place
in any homes as it will only open the door for idle talk
and gossip. Rest assured Satan will continue to do
everything within his power to inject his venom into
those who will give place to him, but we must put on

the whole armor of God and remember Jesus Christ has never lost a battle.

"This I must say to any who might have been involved in any way in this: They are definitely wrong. But there is only one unpardonable sin and that is blasphemy against the Holy Spirit. The Bible says if we confess our sins, he is faithful and just to forgive us our sins and to cleanse us from all unrighteousness." (signed) Brother Nash.

The lawyers continued to batter our pastor with questions to clarify the church's position on healing and medicine. "Reverend Nash," Frazier asked, "when people pray for healing, does healing *always* occur?"

"No . . . it doesn't always happen at that time."

"Does it necessarily happen at some later time?"

"Very definitely . . . at some time . . . ."

"Are you referring to a final healing?"

"Yes."

"Meaning death?"

"Meaning in that day when there will be no more sickness or sorrow, pain or death . . . yes."

"But restricting our discussions to this earthly life, when prayer is offered up for the healing of that particular individual, have you found that it always occurs in this life?"

"Not always . . . ."

Then it was Lee Simmons' turn:

"Reverend Nash," he began stiffly, "you said that the church doesn't think that it is appropriate to do away with medicine as a demonstration of faith; is that correct?"

"I said it was not necessary to do away with it."

"I see. Is it sometimes considered a demonstration of faith to do so?"

"I think each case would have to stand on its own merits."

"So there may be situations, then, in which one of the demonstrations of a person's faith might be to put away his medicine; is that correct?"

"Yes, I think it could be."

"All right, now. Reverend Nash, do you recognize this as being a copy of your denomination's official magazine?" Lee held up an issue of our publication, which had been established in court to contain its doctrines and practices.

"Yes," Pastor Nash answered.

"Okay. Do you see the general topic there, 'Healed of arthritic condition . . .'?" Lee handed the magazine to Pastor Nash.

"Yes."

"I have underlined a phrase there. Would you read that to us, please?"

" 'I had given up the drugs when I came out of the hospital,' " the pastor read. " 'They only hindered God.' "

"Now," Lee pressed, "are these healings asked to be endorsed to verify their authenticity?"

"Yes."

"So you would agree, then, that there are occasions when an individual may be asked by God, or whomever, to demonstrate his faith by not using medication; is that correct?"

"Yes . . . ."

Frazier took advantage of the same line of questioning the next day: "Reverend Nash, there was some discussion that this particular individual had given up drugs, for they only hindered God. Is that the position that your denomination takes with regard to drugs and medicine—that they should be given up, that they only hinder God's work?"

"No, the denomination leaves that up to the individual . . . ."

"Now, in your local church in Barstow, did you teach any of the members of your congregation to do away with medicine prescribed for them by doctors?"

"I don't believe I have ever given this impression . . . ."

"You were here the other day when your wife was testifying about an illness from which she had been healed by faith?"

"Yes, sir."

"Did she from the very start discard doctors and medicine as far as her illness was concerned?"

"No, sir . . . ."

"Now, Reverend Nash, would you think that an individual would be any less faithful if he used medicine?"

"No, it wouldn't necessarily show less faith."

"As far as the church is concerned, then, the acceptance or rejection by an individual of medicine is not a criteria for determining faithfulness, is it?"

"No, sir."

Under further cross examination by Lee Simmons, Pastor Nash summarized his view of faith:

"There is no easy definition of faith, but the Bible calls it 'the substance of things hoped for, the evidence of things not seen.'[1] It's a special gift of God, not something you can work up.

"Jesus said, 'Have the faith of God.'[2] This is the faith

1. Hebrews 11:1.
2. Mark 11:22, "Have faith in God." Literally translated, it is "Have the faith of God."

that accomplished the supernatural. Christ is the author and finisher of our faith.[3] He puts it in us for a specific purpose. If we are the author, He isn't obligated to finish it.

"Sometimes people mistake hope for faith. Hope is an attitude of expectation. Faith *knows* that God will act. In this way it becomes the substance of our hope and the evidence of what we do not see.

"Everything that God does is for our benefit in the body of Christ, not only in this life but in eternity. God has a master plan. The gift of faith can operate only within the program of its Author. Man's faith cannot see beyond the human will. We look at the moment, at the present. He views the future. Divine faith takes this into account. It acts according to His will, it embodies His purpose, it fits into His plan, and it works in His time—all to the glory of God."

Again referring to our denominational magazine, Simmons continued his cross examination.

"I note, Reverend Nash, in this particular article entitled, 'Faith that works,' the story of the centurion coming to Jesus for the healing of his servant. Let me read to you from it:

'. . . How simple yet how wonderful was the centurion's reasoning. He as much as said, 'Lord, if I, an officer, am able to get action when I give a command to my men, then you can, Lord of all the universe, easily speak a

3. Hebrews 12:2.

commanding word to the unseen forces at your disposal and accomplish the healing my servant needs.'

'This is genuine faith illustrated, faith which effected changes in the spiritual realm, faith which recognized the authority of Christ, faith which rested in the power of Christ's word, faith which needed no support from the senses, and it is just such faith any Christian may place in this same Jesus . . . .'

"Reverend Nash, do you recognize that as being an accurate statement of the philosophy and teaching of the church?"

"Yes . . . ."

As the questioning continued at the hands of the prosecutor, Pastor Nash made a statement that shed an all effusive light upon what Lucky and I had done.

"Was there anything about the Parkers' conduct on the day you visited them that deviated from the teachings of the church?" Frazier had asked.

"It would be difficult to give a definite answer on that. People have different ideas of faith or show it in different ways. Sometimes, though, they can get faith and presumption mixed up."

"Well," grinned Frazier, "was there any conduct that you observed in the Parker home that you could characterize as presumption?"

"Let me define what faith and presumption do. Presumption steps beyond proper bounds. It demands . . . rushes ahead of God. *Faith rests.* It leaves the answer in God's hands."

"Did you observe a demanding conduct in the Parker home?" Frazier pressed.

"Yes."

Today, Lucky and I realize we were not at rest during Wesley's travail and death. With minds constantly in a state of confusion, our actions were forced, our confessions hollow. We had claimed the promises of God in vain, ignorant of the conflict between true faith and presumption. We later came to realize that our key error was an act of presumption.

Our understanding of this error developed slowly. The first hurdle was to admit that our approach to faith healing was wrong. It was through much prayer, counseling with Christian leaders, and our own study of the Bible that we came to fully realize the scope of our mistake.

Wesley died needlessly, a victim of our imbalance and misuse of the Bible. We mistook presumption for faith, overstepping the proper bounds of God's sovereign plan for our son's life.

Presumption is putting God between one's foolishness and the painful consequences of his mistaken actions. It is walking by the faith of another instead of obeying the voice of God. It is intimidating God into action against His will. It is applying general Bible verses to specific circumstances without a clear inspiration of God.

Perhaps one of the greatest hindrances to faith, the sin of presumption, is a universal possibility. Even Jesus was tempted by it:

> The devil taketh him up into the holy city, and setteth him on a pinnacle of the temple, and saith unto him, If thou be the Son of God, cast thyself down: for it is written, He shall give

his angels charge concerning thee: and in their hands they shall bear thee up . . . .[4]

In other words the devil sneered, "Go ahead. If You're the Son of God, jump off. I dare you. God will protect You. He won't let You down. He'll honor His Word."

Jesus' response is significant. He said, "It is written again, 'Thou shalt not *tempt* the Lord thy God.' "[5] An alternate reading says, "Thou shalt not put the Lord . . . to the *test.*" Unwittingly, that's what Lucky and I did.

We acted presumptuously by trying to "prove" God and our faith. Not understanding the command of Jesus against putting Him to the test, we were ignorantly trying to force God into the position of acting against His sovereign will.

In Malachi 3:10 God says, "Bring the whole tithe into the storehouse, so that there may be food in My house, and test Me now in this . . . if I will not open for you the windows of heaven, and pour out for you a blessing until there is no more need."

How does this passage reconcile with "Thou shalt not put the Lord . . . to the *test*"?

We can test God only *when* He specifically asks us to do so. This is where we made our mistake. God did not tell us to withhold Wesley's insulin to prove His faithfulness and our faith, as we had assumed.

A major flaw exists in the *positive confession* principle that is so popular today. The practice encourages people to incorporate selected verses from the Bible as

4. Matthew 4:5,6.
5. Matthew 4:7.

their own record or promise from God. Passages concerned with many spiritual principles can have general application. But not all verses necessarily will apply to your circumstances or God's plan for your life. While the Bible is true and its promises can be claimed, one cannot arbitrarily take some passages and say, "I'm going to stand on them."

This was a painful lesson for Lucky and I to learn.

The promises of God must be given; that is, inspired by the Holy Spirit to a person for a specific need. Only when God speaks to us clearly, applying His Word to our circumstances, can we stand upon them, for it is then that God's gift of faith begins to flow on our behalf.

Arbitrarily claiming the general promises of the Bible for specific needs opens the door to presumption. *Out of balance*, many of the teachings of the Bible can have heartbreaking consequences.

In their zeal people often have taken spiritual insights and transformed them into formulas. "If you follow these steps," they argue, "God must honor His Word."

Formulas in themselves are not evil. Often they are heavenly prescriptions for someone's ailing finances, poor health or crumbling marriage. They can be the result of God's inspiration for an individual's need. Philippians 4:6-8 was Lucky's "prescription for sanity." It says:

> Be anxious for nothing, but in everything by prayer and supplication with thanksgiving let your requests be made known to God.
> And the peace of God, which surpasses all comprehension, shall *guard* your hearts and

your minds in Christ Jesus.

Finally, brethren, whatever is true, whatever is honorable, whatever is right, whatever is pure, whatever is lovely, whatever is of good repute, if there is any excellence and if anything worthy of praise, let your mind dwell on these things.[6]

This passage was given to her to meet a specific need during the heartbreaking hours of our ordeal when Satan bombarded her with guilt and thoughts of unworthiness and shame. By following the instructions of these verses, she discovered a formula for "guarding" her mind against the enemy.

To another person in similar circumstances, the Holy Spirit might inspire a different verse. Problems arise when a formula is presented as an absolute for others to follow. Too often it becomes a straight jacket of legalism. When the formula doesn't work, the individual is troubled with guilt and his faith weakened.

Formulas have helped people to exercise faith for miracles. Yet dangers exist with the general use of spiritual recipes. People tend to work the formula instead of seeking God. Formulas sometimes put God in a box, implying what He will do everytime in a given situation. Formulas often elevate man; we have finally figured out how God works, making it possible for us to manipulate Him as we please.

Formulas are tempting because they appear to offer simple solutions. When we read God's word on a daily

6. Philippians 4:6-8.

basis, He can say more to us. When we rely on a formula as a substitute for reading His Word, we limit His communication and sometimes violate His sovereignty.

Lucky and I claimed the promises of God for Wesley's healing, but our son died. Presumption, in the guise of faith, kept us from seeing the sovereign time and method of God. By taking Wesley off his insulin, we in effect were forcing God to heal our son. God has many varieties of healing. By our act we prevented His perfect method for Wesley's life. God cannot answer "faith" that is rooted in presumption and which maneuvers Him into acting against His sovereign will.

One cannot live by another person's faith. An illustration of this is recorded in Matthew 14:22-33. Jesus' disciples were caught in a storm at sea, and their boat was being battered by the waves. Suddenly in the night, He came walking toward them upon the water.

"It's a ghost!" the fishermen cried in horror.

"Take courage, it is I," Jesus called. "Do not be afraid."

"If it's You, Lord, command me to come to You on the water," Peter challenged.

"Come!"

Peter climbed out of the boat and walked on the water to Jesus. Peter's faith, set ablaze by a word from the Lord, enabled him to do the impossible. *But*, the fisherman didn't get out of the boat until Jesus said "Come." Had Jesus said nothing, and Peter climbed out of the boat, he could have drowned.

I had been taught to "strike out for that deep water of faith", and one can—if they're called. Christ's word to Peter was meant for him alone. Had the other disciples presumed upon the same word, they would likely have perished.

In a way this is a mirror of our error. God had not said "come" in our instance. We took it upon ourselves to enter those deep waters.

How can we know when Jesus says, "Come" or when the Holy Spirit quickens a verse to meet our need? The Apostle Paul wrote that "the letter killeth, but the Spirit giveth life."[7] The inspiration of the Spirit is unmistakable. A quickened Bible verse suddenly springs to life; it bursts into your understanding like a beautiful, fragrant flower. No question about it! The passage is a clear message from God, for it takes on a new dimension as it speaks to your circumstance. You just *know* that the Lord has spoken. The faith of God swells within, and you march confidently, triumphantly ahead.

The Bible says, "Faith cometh by hearing, and hearing by the Word of God."[8] This faith is a gift.[9] There's no great mystery in it. It comes so often in the Christian's life that prayers are answered and needs are met without a conscious awareness of its operation.

Weymouth calls the gift "special faith" in his translation of the word in 1 Corinthians 12. Coneybeare translates it "wonder-working faith." H.A.W. Meyers reads, "heroic faith," and James Moffatt reads, "The gift of faith." Since this faith is not natural to the human heart, its function makes it a gift from God.

Faith becomes evident in times of need. Hardly a day goes by when someone doesn't need healing, finan-

7. 2 Corinthians 3:6.
8. Romans 10:17.
9. 1 Corinthians 12:8-10.

cial solutions, guidance, strength, peace of mind or wisdom.

We can go to God's Word for a reassuring promise to cover the need, but it's the Holy Spirit's function to direct us to the verse that meets the situation. Therefore, we must allow God to control this step.

Peter heard the word of the Lord. He had no doubt that Jesus had spoken. Faith is not just believing; it is knowing the will, purpose, and timing of God. With such knowledge and inspiration, we can claim the promises of God.

When the gift of faith is operating, calm peace will prevail. We'll experience the rest of faith (Hebrews 4:8-10), having the assurance that everything is all right (Isaiah 3:10).

Our task is to put our complete confidence in the sovereignty of God. When faith is present, answers come. Battles are won. Spiritual mountains crumble. Impossibilities become possibilities. But when faith is absent, nothing happens. Confidence erodes, desperation sets in; anxiety, pressure, stress, doubt, and fear produce struggle.

Realizing that the verses we claimed were not God-given in our situation was another painful experience to us. Indeed, they were an expression of our human desires. So desperate was our hope for Wesley's healing—and later his resurrection—that we were blinded to Satan's deception.

Our experience has taught us that God sovereignly heals whom He chooses. Any genuine faith healing can stand the test of medical verification. Whether or not a cure takes place as the result of prayer, God must decide. All healing comes from God—medicine, nature, and prayer are methods by which He accomplishes it. It is presumptive to believe a healing has taken place when the symptoms persist.

Too often Christians misuse the verse in 1 Peter 2:24, ". . . by whose stripes ye *were* healed." Confessing this Scripture, some people run around saying, "I'm healed, I'm healed," while they continue to suffer. This is what we did with Wesley. But if the healing is real, the symptoms will disappear.

Often healing is progressive. It's okay to say "I'm being healed" while continuing to treat symptoms medically. But it is a lie to say that we're cured when suffering persists. Until our miracle comes, we can treat the illness without compromising faith.

The marvelous discoveries of medical science could not have come apart from God. It is ridiculous to assume that medicine necessarily will thwart divine healing—unless God for His own sovereign purpose has called us to rely solely on faith for healing.

The question is not whether God heals. The controversy is over the means. Whatever method *He chooses* lies within the prerogative of God. Ample evidence exists in the Bible for the cooperation between medicine and healing by faith.

Everything lies within the sovereign will of God—that is, events take place within *His perfect methods and timing*. Wesley went to an untimely death because we stepped beyond this limit. Had we continued his medical treatment, we may have eventually discovered God's more perfect plan for our son. It doesn't matter what method God uses, the results are still the same. Jesus remains the Healer!

Knowing that God heals through His own methods and timing has given Lucky and me a more balanced view.

During our trial as Pastor Nash spoke of faith, I was yet to admit that my approach to healing was wrong. Bewildered and feeling guilty for our son's death, I clung tenaciously to my hope of his resurrection. Pastor Nash's words, "faith rests," haunted me through that week and into the next, when Lucky and I began to testify on our own behalf. It was then that my mind began to rest.

The first hurdle on the long run to corrective re-learning was about to be jumped.

12

As the World Waits

The early morning sun shone dully through the residue of the previous day's smog, casting a false, alpen glow over the houses that made up Lois Brown's neighborhood.

My stomach and throat hurt. Remembering Tom Frazier's biting cross examination of the day before made me feel even more apprehensive. Today, I would again be on the witness stand.

What I had discovered last night would change the course of my testimony—perhaps even the trial. How could I relate this exciting new understanding of our actions to the court? Would the jury be sympathetic? Would the prosecutor distort what would be said and use it against me?

I recalled how it had happened. I was reading a book by Corrie ten Boom called *Marching Orders for the End Battle*. A statement in her book seemed to leap off the page: "When the devil cannot keep us back, he tries to push us so fast that we exaggerate. Then we are in danger of forgetting to love."

"Forgetting to love." The words penetrated deeply. Suddenly, everything Lucky had been saying about our lack of love made sense. We had allowed what we thought was faith to overshadow love. My heart ached as I recalled how much we had wanted to give Wesley his insulin, to end his pain. I would have given anything at that moment to drown the sounds of his agony. Yet, fearful of failing the test of faith and thereby displeasing God, we had closed our minds to his suffering.

The Bible's teaching on love now began to come into sharp focus:

> Now abide faith, hope, love . . . but the greatest of these is love.
> In Christ Jesus neither circumcision nor un-circumcision means anything, but faith working through love.[1]

A sense of joy and relief swept through me as the truth began to dawn. Love is greater than faith. *Faith works through love.* The measure of all action must be love. God's chief motivation for healing—or not healing—is love.

That was it—that first big hurdle that I needed to leap. Now it was clear to me where we had gone wrong in our approach to healing by faith. As I pondered this, my understanding seemed to expand rapidly—as though the truth was being flashed into my mind: We had pitted faith against love.

Any action we take that is contrary to love must be re-examined, even if we think it is an act of faith. Love is the controlling factor in faith that is authored by

1. 1 Corinthians 13:13; Galatians 5:6.

God. Love had told us to give Wesley the insulin and end his agony. What we mistook for faith demanded that we resist the "temptation" to give insulin and continue to "prove" God.

I had looked upon our battle between love and faith in the light of Abraham's willingness to sacrifice his only son, Isaac. Abraham built an altar and laid upon it the kindling wood for burning the sacrifice. He bound Isaac and laid him on the altar upon the wood. Knife clenched firmly in his fist, Abraham poised it high above the trusting form of his son, ready for the plunge of death. So complete was the man of God's faith that he was willing to sacrifice the dearest love of his life.

Suddenly, a voice boomed out of Heaven. "Abraham, Abraham! Do not stretch out your hand against the lad . . . for now I know that you fear God . . ."[2]

Surely the Lord was testing us in the same manner. We never believed that Wess would die; the Lord just wanted us to be willing to go to the brink. Like Isaac's rescue, Wesley would be healed at the last moment, when we had proven our faithfulness to God.

The nature of love is so beautifully portrayed in the Bible. It is patient and kind. Never envious, it doesn't boil over with jealousy. Love is not conceited—arrogant and inflated with pride; it is not rude, and does not act unbecomingly. God's love in us doesn't insist on its own rights, for it is not self-seeking; it is not touchy, fretful, or resentful; it pays no attention to a suffered wrong. It rejoices when right and truth prevail, not at

2. Genesis 22:1-12.

injustice and unrighteousness. Love bears up under
anything and everything that comes, is always ready to
believe the best of every person, its hopes are fadeless
under all circumstances, and it endures everything
without weakening. Love never fails—never fades out,
becomes obsolete, or comes to an end.[3]

The greatest power that God can give us is love. It's
not the kind of power that raises bumps on the skin or
explodes inside with some electrifying experience. But
it works wonders. Such love is a gentle flow of
tenderness and concern.

Jesus is the perfect example of this love. Once a leper
came to Him for healing. "And Jesus, *moved with
compassion*, put forth his hand and cleansed the
leper."[4]

Love motivated Jesus when He taught: "And Jesus,
when he came out, saw much people, and was *moved
with compassion* toward them . . . and He began to
teach them."[5]

When He saw that the thousands who had traveled a
long distance to hear Him were hungry, He said, "I
have *compassion* on the multitude."[6]

When the Lord saw the widow grieving over the
death of her only son, "He had *compassion* on her, and
said unto her 'Weep not.' And he came and touched
the bier . . . and he said, 'Young man, I say unto thee,
Arise.' And he that was dead sat up, and began to
speak. And he delivered him to his mother."[7]

3. 1 Corinthians 13:4-8.
4. Mark 1:41.
5. Mark 6:34.
6. Mark 8:1-9.
7. Luke 7:11-15.

Jesus had compassion because people mattered to Him. He wasn't interested in projects, or contests, or traditions. It didn't matter to Him where people were socially; whether they were rich or poor; good looking or ugly. He saw people as people. When they hurt, He healed them; when they suffered, He delivered them; when they grieved, He comforted them. And when they rejoiced, He laughed with them.

In my place, what would Jesus have done for Wesley? In the light of His great love, the answer was a painful one to consider.

Jesus said, "It is not those who are healthy who need a physician, but those who are ill. But go and learn what this means, 'I desire compassion (mercy), and not sacrifice' . . . If you had known what this means . . . you would not have condemned the innocent."[8]

In withholding insulin from Wesley, we had offered up a difficult sacrifice of faith. Blindly standing upon God's Word, we could not see this truth: Mercy comes above sacrifice. Had Abraham ignored the voice of the Lord and plunged the knife into Isaac's heart, he would have committed no greater sin than we. It was mercy that echoed from above and rescued a trusting Isaac. That voice could not clearly speak to us because we had been deafened by our zeal for faith.

Today in looking back on our ordeal, I understand why I clung so desperately to the hope that Wesley would return. I couldn't cope with the guilt that ac-

8. Matt. 9:12, 13; 12:7.

companied such a convicting lesson. As long as the possibility of Wesley's resurrection remained in my mind, I could hold back the crippling grief that was sure to come. Having now reconciled that Wesley is gone, we still have that hope, for one day "the dead in Christ shall rise, then we which are alive and remain shall be caught up together in the clouds to meet the Lord in the air: And so shall we ever be with the Lord. Wherefore comfort one another with these words."[9]

God's love toward Lucky and me through the hot and cold of this severe trial was amazing. Peering through our ignorance to view sincerety, He spoke the truth to our hearts in love and led us slowly out of error and sin. At first we confused the peace we felt as approval for our actions. But it wasn't that at all. His grace was so tender that even in our wrong He comforted us. He gave us peace not because we were right, but simply because He cared for us.

The court proceedings on my second day of testimony got underway with my attorney doing the questioning. I took advantage of the opportunity to share some of my new insights.

"Now, Mr. Parker," Bill Russler began, "considering everything that's happened, do you believe that the Lord has failed you?"

"No."

"At the time of Wesley's death, did you think that you were doing wrong?"

"No."

9. 1 Thessalonians 4:16-18.

Spectators in the gallery began to murmur.

"What is your feeling today?"

"We were wrong in some of the things we did."

"Do you believe you should have given Wesley insulin?"

"Objection—leading," Frazier's annoyed voice interrupted.

"Sustained," Judge Williams agreed. Then turning to Bill, he instructed, "You can ask what the specifics were without directing the answer."

"Very well," Bill shrugged. Turning back to me, he resumed. "Do you consider today that there are some things you should have done which you did not do?"

"Yes."

"What do you consider that you should have done?"

"We should have administered the insulin to eliminate the suffering while we continued to trust God for Wesley's healing."

The muffled sounds of the gallery quieted, every ear straining to catch my carefully chosen words.

"Your wife's view, as expressed from the witness stand, was somewhat similar to yours; is that correct?"

"Yes."

"Did you come to this view at the same time your wife did?"

"No, it was several months later. I have been praying about it for many months, and last night I was reading a book by Corrie ten Boom . . . ." I shared briefly the meaning of love that had been opened to me, then concluded, ". . . to maintain faith, we forgot love. I see now that was a mistake. Our love should have overruled what we thought we were required to do."

Bill nodded and turned to the judge. "Your Honor, I have no further questions."

After court was adjourned, Lucky and I filed out of the room with our lawyers, exhausted, and looking forward to a weekend of rest.

With just a few more days of testimony, the jury retired to deliberate our case. I was relieved that the brutal questioning was over.

On our long drive home, Lucky and I sat quietly, each wrapped in our own thoughts. The more altitude we gained through the pass, the lighter our load felt. The air seemed fresher and clearer, the sun brighter, the fleecy clouds on the horizon whiter.

I remembered one of the last statements Russler had made in his summation. Standing before the jury, gesturing dramatically, he said emotionally, ". . . and after coming to know this man, Lawrence Parker, I can say that without a doubt, even if you vote him guilty, he will be able to leave this courtroom with head held high . . . ."

Judge Williams had been fair. Lucky and I felt comfortable with the jury. Still, a big question remained: How would they decide our case? The prosecutor had sought to destroy us. Our attorneys had fought long and hard to gain our freedom. But how would the jury weigh the evidence?

As the world awaited the verdict, we stepped into our home that evening determined to let the future rest in God's hands.

13

"Guilty"

After enduring thirteen long weeks of trial, we waited an additional six days for the jury to reach its decision. Hastily called into the courtroom when the verdict had been reached, Lucky and I sat nervously at the Counselors' table.

Finally, the jurors—twelve men and women—filed in one by one. I searched each face for clues to our future. Most looked down, avoiding my gaze.

Judge Williams entered the court, and the session began. "This is the People versus Parker and Parker," he intoned. "The record will reflect the jurors are all present and in their places. The defendants are present with Counsel."

Turning to the jury, he asked, "Has the jury arrived at verdicts in this case?"

The foreman, a woman named Jan Hoover, nervously glanced toward Lucky and me.

"Yes, Your Honor," she answered.

"Will you hand all the verdict forms to the bailiff, please?"

Jan handed the small sheaf of papers to the bailiff, who in turn gave them to the judge. The sounds of restless feet and nervous coughs interrupted the silence as he reviewed the verdicts, then handed the papers to the clerk.

Judge Williams again spoke: "Mr. Parker will rise . . ."

I stood, trembling inside, my heart pounding hard and fast. News reporters in the gallery braced themselves, pens poised to record the jury's decision.

". . . and the court clerk will read the verdicts."

Her voice was distinct as she began to read. "In the Superior Court of the State of California for the County of San Bernardino, the People versus Lawrence Elsworth Parker and Alice Elizabeth Parker, defendants. We, the jury, find the defendant, Lawrence Elsworth Parker, guilty of the crime of . . . ."

As the clerk droned on, the word echoed endlessly in my mind: "Guilty . . . guilty . . . guilty . . . ." I glanced helplessly at the jury—some were quietly weeping, the others sitting solemnly. I wanted to reach out to them and say, "Hey, it's okay. You did the best you could. Don't feel bad."

The clerk finished reading, and it was Lucky's turn to stand. The verdict for her was the same—guilty on all counts.

As the judge addressed the jury, his voice was kindly and sympathetic. "Ladies and gentlemen of the jury, this now concludes your services in this case. I realize that this has been a long and difficult trial and that your deliberations were careful. Few cases have been of such duration in this county, few where jurors were called upon to make more difficult decisions than you had to make. My decision in sentencing will be equally difficult . . . . You may be excused."

As the jury slowly filed through the door they had entered, Judge Williams turned his attention to the Counselors' table.

"What do you wish to do with respect to pronouncement of judgment?"

"He means your sentencing," Bill Russler whispered in my ear.

"Your Honor," Lee Simmons began as he rose, "we would at this time make application for probation and ask that the matter be referred to the Probation Department for that purpose."

For the next few minutes we went through the tedious process of setting the date of sentence, making application for probation and requesting a new trial.

"Applications for probation received," Judge Williams intoned. "The matter is referred to the Probation Office for an investigation and report. The report shall be furnished to Counsel not less than five days prior to the time for pronouncement of judgment . . . . The hearing on the motion for a new trial will be set at the same time."

"My client is now on her own recognizance," Lee said. "May she remain so during that period?"

"Yes, so ordered."

Bill repeated the request for me. The judge waved the answer, then adjourned the court. As we rose to leave, I turned to see that the court reporter for the San Bernardino Sun-Telegram had covered his eyes with sunglasses. Perhaps it was to conceal the deep emotion he felt. He had been to every court session, and his articles had been unbiased. Half way to the exit, he stopped us.

"Excuse me, Mr. and Mrs. Parker," His voice was apologetic. "I realize this isn't a good time to ask you for a statement, but I have to print something tomorrow. Is there anything you'd like me to say?"

I appreciated that. He wanted to print what *we*

wanted. Nervously, he shifted his weight from one foot to the other as he awaited our answer. As if to end the embarrassing silence, he continued.

"I didn't know how emotionally involved I was in this case until I heard the verdict. I wanted to hear a 'not guilty' decision. I'm sorry . . . ." His voice cracked.

I put my hand on his arm. "That's okay. The jury did the best job it could. Just write that we're really tired, and glad the trial is over. And that . . . well, that I'm just thankful that I've got Jesus to lean on. If I didn't have Him, I wouldn't make it out of here."

Writing in a little notebook, the reporter finished taking my statement, looked up and smiled wryly. "Thank you, Mr. Parker. Good luck."

Accompanied by Russler, we entered the hallway and twisted our way through the maze of whirring cameras, glaring lights and shouting reporters. "What do you think of the verdict?" When we finally made it to his office and closed the door, I collapsed in the nearest chair—physically and emotionally drained.

"Vultures!" Lucky hissed. "They're nothing but a bunch of vultures." At that, she began to sob uncontrollably.

To this day I am amazed at how God miraculously comforted us as we awaited our sentences.

Lucky and I spent the night of our verdict at Lois Brown's house to compose ourselves before going home. She took us with her to church. Losing the hope that we would not be convicted, Lucky felt desperate and depressed. Her mind in a whirl of confusion and anxiety over our future, she struggled to focus on the evangelist's message. Suddenly, the words "someone here has had a great disappointment" penetrated her turmoil.

"Disappointment" is an understatement, she fretted in self-pity. The preacher gave an invitation to prayer, and Lucky made her way slowly to the altar and knelt. As the pianist played the hymn *I'll Go Where You Want Me to God, Dear Lord* she cried, "Not that, Lord. Don't ask me to go to prison." Unable to verbalize her agony, she wept uncontrollably until she felt released from her pent-up tensions and the Holy Spirit had ministered to her in the manner of Romans 8:26 and 27:

> . . . the Spirit also helps our weakness; for we do not know how to pray as we should, but the Spirit Himself intercedes for us with groanings too deep for words; and He who searches the heart knows what the mind of the Spirit is, because He intercedes for the saints according to the will of God.

Experiencing this gave her more confidence in God's promise in Romans 8:28 that all things would work out for our good.

After the service, the evangelist comforted her. "You've been going through a long, desolate valley, and the Lord wants you to know that you're almost out of it." She took refuge in those words.

At home the next morning I stared at the headline in The Sun-Telegram

Parkers found guilty
in their son's death

Pamela saw the pain on my face caused by the announcement. She quietly sat beside me on the couch and tenderly put her arm around my shoulder. Without a word she had said, "Dad, it's okay. I love you."

The Lord had chosen to comfort me through my daughter.

Another source of encouragement came just five days before we were to be sentenced. The Probation Department recommended to Judge Williams that we be given probation instead of a prison term. We could have been given up to twenty-five years for the crimes of which we were convicted.

We came to court that Friday morning firmly convinced that God had worked out the most equitable sentence possible. The tension began to build inside me as we sat waiting for the proceedings to begin. Everything seemed the same as it had been during the trial, except that the jury box was empty. Some of the jurors were in the gallery box now—a few had been called as witnesses for Lee's motion for a mistrial; others were there out of curiosity. A couple of reporters also were present. A television camera had been set up in the hallway—again blinding lights piercing our eyes as we had walked past. Pam and Pat sat near us, wide-eyed and frightened by the crowd. We had been advised by Lee to bring them.

Finally the judge entered and sat down at his bench. He shuffled some papers, then looked up. I glanced at my watch: 9:30 a.m.

"People versus Lawrence Elsworth Parker and Alice Elizabeth Parker," he spoke solemnly, looking to the Counselors' table.

"Ready for Lawrence Parker," Russler intoned.

"Ready for Alice Parker," chimed Simmons.

"People are ready," said Frazier.

"Very well. Will Counsel please approach the bench?"

Before the judge, the attorneys held a lengthy, whispered discussion. Later I learned that they had questioned the wisdom of having our girls present. The judge overruled Frazier's objections and allowed them to remain.

"We will first proceed to hear the arguments of Counsel and consider any evidence that may be produced with reference to the motion for a new trial . . . ."

Our attorney's call for a mistrial stemmed from an incident during jury deliberation. The bailiff had given the jury a dictionary for the purpose of looking up the meaning of some words about which there was considerable confusion. Bill and Lee contended that this was misconduct on the part of the jury because it was seeking advice and counsel from parties outside the jury room. The testimony and arguments for and against the motion for a new trial dragged on for hours.

Finally, Judge Williams made a ruling: "It was distressing for the Court to hear of the misconduct of the bailiff and of the jury . . . . But I have looked at the definitions, listened to the testimony, and compared those definitions with the instructions that were given, and I see no likelihood that they have prejudicially affected the verdict.

"It is not likely that a different result would be reached if, in fact, a new trial was granted . . . . The motion for a new trial made on behalf of each of the defendants is hereby denied."

Lee stood quickly, looking as though he had expected the ruling all along.

"Your Honor, this is the time and place set for pronouncement of judgment."

"The Court has received, read, and considered the report of the probation officer relating to each of the defendants," the judge began. "In essence, the reports are the same except for the defendant's comments . . . . Do you waive formal arraignment for pronouncement of judgment?"

Our attorneys said yes.

"Do you have any legal cause why judgment should not now be pronounced?"

"No, Your Honor," they answered, Lee praising the thoroughness of the probation report.

"Thank you, Mr. Simmons." Judge Williams then directed his attention to the prosecutor. "Mr. Frazier?"

Since our verdict had been handed down nearly two months ago, Frazier had been relatively quiet compared to his performance in court. I had an uneasy feeling, however, that he had been smouldering under that cool exterior. He exploded into such a vindictive attack on us that our children left the courtroom.

"Your Honor, the defendants in this case acted in such a manner that their conduct resulted in the death of their son. I think that is a tragic thing to occur, but it is more significant in that he died at the hands of the *parents* and that there are additional children resident in this home."

Frazier's eyes flashed in anger. "The probation report indicates the numerous people interviewed as a result of the investigation feel that Mr. and Mrs. Parker are good parents. Yet I cannot help but ponder—what is a good parent? One that would permit such a thing to come to pass? The Court must certainly keep in mind the fact of the other children remaining in the home and any possibility of harm or injury occurring to them."

He also accused us of having no remorse. I was flabbergasted at his speech, suddenly remembering something that may have triggered his unkind attack: We had been asked to comment on the kind of sentence we should serve. Anything that the court would decide would be equitable and just, I had said. Lucky, however, had written that any sentence of the court would probably do no good, meaning that she could suffer no greater punishment than the death of her son. I shook my head at what the deputy district attorney had mistaken for a lack of remorse.

Frazier continued to harangue us, strongly recommending that we be detained in a mental diagnostic facility.

Russler leaned over to me and grumbled in disgust, "My God, what does he want you to do—go about in public in sackcloth and ashes for the rest of your lives? He's already won the case. What else does he want?"

The prosecutor continued his tirade, "We are talking about something very serious that has occurred in this case . . . . We have a human life that has been lost here. It is not something that should be taken lightly . . . ."

As Frazier finished, Simmons began his equally fiery rebuttle. "Perhaps the greatest understatement that's ever been made in this court is that this is a serious case. That is an incredible statement. Anyone who could read the letter of Mrs. Parker and say that they have no remorse for the death of their son has no sensitivity at all . . . .

"It occurs to me that very little can be done to them that, frankly, would be any greater than what they had done to themselves. I believe that the recommendation of the Probation Department is in order, and I would ask that the Court abide by it. Thank you."

My attorney joined Lee's defense of the report. And judging by the reactions of the newsmedia, curious spectators and former jurors in the gallery, it seemed that Frazier stood alone. As the judge prepared to give sentence, Lucky and I were fearful. We were uncertain how the prosecutor's speech may have affected him.

Judge Williams began sonorously, carefully: "I believe the defendants, unlike many others who have appeared before me, do have an understanding that what they did was wrong, and I do believe that there has been remorse on their part, and that they are, on a day-to-day basis, together with the members of their family, experiencing the loss of a child that had once been with them.

"They most certainly are guilty. The jury that prayerfully deliberated this case arrived at that judgment. However, I am sure that the defendants feel that they have the Lord's forgiveness, and without presuming on His mercy, I hope that such is the case.

"Filling the responsibility that the Court has to the defendants and to society, I consider that probation is appropriate. It should be meaningful and individualized. I have confidence with the very thorough investigation and report in this case that it will be treated differently than many probation cases."

I was relieved as the judge began to read my sentence.

"Pronouncement of judgment is hereby withheld

for the offense of involuntary manslaughter, a felony, and for the offense of child abuse, a felony, offenses for which this defendant now stands convicted.

"The defendant, Lawrence Elsworth Parker, is granted probation for a period of five years under the following terms and conditions . . . ."

I was to violate no law, report to the probation officer once a month, cooperate in a plan of rehabilitation, and maintain employment. I couldn't leave the state without permission nor change my residence or employment without the approval of the probation officer. I was to receive eighty hours of psychological care at the High Desert Mental Health Clinic in Barstow and serve four hundred hours in a work sentence program there. If anyone of my family suffered an injury or illness that confined any member to home or bed, this had to be reported. And I was not to advise, suggest or infer to anyone that he should not seek or follow medical advice.

"Are you willing to accept probation on those conditions?"

"Yes, I am."

As the judge began to read Lucky's sentence, I sighed with relief. At least we wouldn't go to prison. Her probation was the same as mine, except she wasn't expected to find a job.

I glanced briefly at Frazier sitting sullenly next to me at the Counselor's table. Our sentences had served as a mild rebuke to his performance that day, for he had gone beyond the bounds of duty and turned vicious. So much had happened since nine-thirty that morning. I looked at my watch. It was nearly 6:15 p.m.

Judge Williams then began to wind down the proceedings:

"That will take care of matters, except for the recital of the appeal rights, which the Court is obliged to make at this time . . . .

"Mr. and Mrs. Parker, it is my duty to advise you of your right to appeal to the Appellate Court from the judgment of this Court . . . ."

Finishing a lengthy list of rules and regulations governing appeals, the judge asked, "Do you understand your rights of appeal as I have explained them to you, Mr. Parker?"

"Yes, sir."

"Mrs. Parker?"

"Yes."

As Judge Williams rose and exited through the door behind the bench, everyone else in the courtroom stood in respect. Frazier hurriedly stuffed papers into his briefcase and quickly stalked out, brushing past reporters as he went. Lucky and I shook hands with our lawyers, happy that the ordeal was over.

As we drove home that evening, an appeal seemed the right course for our future. Our lawyers knew what was best. They planned on it from the start. Simmons had actually addressed the Appellate Court during our trial, believing that he would take the case possibly all the way to the Supreme Court.

As we had walked out of the courtroom that day, Russler had asked, "Larry, you *are* going to appeal, aren't you?"

"Yes," I had replied, surprised. "Isn't that what we had planned all along?"

Two weeks later I received a jolting phone call from Lee. "Larry, I'm sorry to bother you like this . . . ."

"That's okay, Lee. What's up?"

"Well, it's about the appeal. If you and Lucky want

me to represent you, you'll have to come up with three
thousand dollars, or I just won't be able to swing it . . . ."

"I'm sorry, Lee, we don't have three thousand
dollars right now. We'll have to pray about it. I'll call
you later."

Hanging up the phone, I flushed with shame. We
hadn't even considered whether the Lord wanted us to
appeal. Lucky and I agreed that night to seek God's
will in this matter.

Three factors finally influenced our decision.

First, the division caused by the trial among the
body of Christ. Pastor Nash had been sided against us
by the media, protecting his congregation and
denomination from the slurs they might receive
because of the publicity. Christian friends who had
been summoned to testify against us feared we would
no longer want them as friends. It was apparent
through the media and the mail we had received that
other Christians nationwide had chosen sides, for and
against. It was not a pretty sight—the body of Christ in
disunity, many bitter over our actions. If disharmony
existed now, what would it be like after another trial,
and another, and another?

Second, the wisdom of a Bible verse we had received
from Dick Mills nearly a year ago: "The Lord shall
fight for you and ye shall *hold your peace.*" If our
lawyers were to petition on our behalf, we really
wouldn't be holding our peace, we reasoned.

Third, the pastor of the Victorville church counseled
us against the appeal.

I called Lee with the news.

"Hello, Lee? Larry. About the appeal. I've decided
to drop it."

"What?" demanded Lee. "But . . . you can't stop it

now! Hey, if it's the money, forget it. I'll defend you for free."

"No, no," I interrupted politely. "It's just that we have prayed and sought spiritual counsel over this, and I believe that the Lord would have me withdraw the appeal."

Lee tried to reason with me for several minutes, but my decision was final. We hung up quietly. Lucky and I would get down to living a normal life again—as normal as it could be for a pair of felons.

14

A New Beginning

The coordinator of the Care-line at the High Desert Mental Health Clinic seemed uneasy in our presence as we arrived to begin our sentences. Because of the stigma that surrounded us, it took time to win the confidence of the staff.

As required by the court, we began to see a psychologist. Our first session was therapeutic. He asked painful questions about Wesley's death, perhaps thinking it would be cleansing for us to express how we felt. I liked the man—he almost seemed apologetic that he had re-opened our hurts. Yet it helped.

After that first visit, we would just talk about whatever came to our minds. One session was spent on solar energy. I suppose he had been satisfied with our mental health after our initial contact and continued the counseling only to fulfill the sentences.

Lucky and I also underwent training for our work on the Care-line, a crisis hotline-referral service. We learned how to listen and to draw from people the information that was needed to refer them to another agency. This was amusing to me because some of these techniques had been used on us by the psychologists who interviewed Lucky and me before the trial.

The clinic staff had us doing a variety of other tasks that counted as community service. Lucky did secretarial work, answered the phones, even worked on a patchwork carpet that one of the workers had begun to brighten the dreary office. I helped with odd jobs, even put down a metal runner for the carpet. Our probation officer was willing to credit almost anything against our work-sentences.

Unfortunately, the board of the mental health clinic would not allow us to serve as telephone workers on the Care-line for fear of community opinion. Much prejudice existed against our mental stability, and they questioned our effectiveness to help people.

The clinic was disappointed at the board's decision. The staff needed volunteers desperately, and we had shown promise during our training. Nevertheless we were relieved. Although it would have been rewarding in many ways, working on this secular hotline could have been frustrating. We were trained mainly to be a sounding board, to refer people to agencies that could give the callers more in-depth help. But it would compromise our convictions to refer a young, pregnant girl to a county health agency where she would possibly be advised to have an abortion. I could see how this service could be of greater value if we could present Christ as an integral part of a solution to the caller's problems. But we could not have helped any person who called with what we considered a moral or spiritual problem. Mentioning Jesus or religion was strictly taboo.

Our probation officer accepted many volunteer projects in fulfillment of our community service. Lucky worked in his office interviewing others on probation for various types of government funded jobs. He also counted her work at the school library and at a Christian bookstore. The publicity of our trial drew a lot of mail from people with similar problems. Our probation officer accepted my letters of reply as a community effort. He even credited an article I wrote for a religious magazine about the lessons we had learned through our ordeal.

With our children in school, Lucky was able to work off her four hundred hours of volunteer service at a rapid pace. It was difficult for me to meet that quota because of my job. On my appeal and recommendation of the probation officer, my hours were cut in half, and the judge said he would consider terminating the probation early. That one thought made my volunteer work more enjoyable.

Meanwhile, Lee Simmons had been elected municipal court judge in Barstow. He wanted to establish a service directing people to various assignments in the community and asked us to coordinate it as part of our sentence. We would contact various public agencies to ask them if they needed volunteers. If a person couldn't pay for a traffic violation or misdemeanor, Judge Simmons would allow him to work for one of these agencies on a referral from us. People who could more than afford to pay their fines qualified for the program also. Lee believed they needed to be reprimanded in a way they would not soon forget.

The program was convenient for us because we could coordinate it from our home. We enjoyed working with Lee and the Probation Department to help these people. After I completed my reduced sentence, someone else was given the responsibility for its coordination. Although it had been a fulfilling—and successful—community project, I was glad it was over, for that divorced us from the constant reminder of our probation.

Other stipulations of our sentences remained. We had to meet with the probation officer once a month, and we couldn't leave the state without written permission. The latter hindered us on occasions from picking up friends at the airport in Las Vegas. Once we were in San Diego and wanted to take an excursion into Tijuana, Mexico. But we hadn't had the foresight to get a permission slip. Most of us take our freedoms for granted until we find ourselves limited or restricted. It's frustrating to know you're confined, even in the great outdoors.

Throughout the days of our trial and probation, Lucky and I had a prevailing confidence that things would work out to our good. Romans 8:28—"God causes all things to work together for good to those who love God"—sustained us through many difficult times. One series of events stands clear in my memory.

It was during our trial. Terminated from work, because my leave of absence had stretched beyond my employer's limit, we were without definite income. Nevertheless, the Lord had been supplying our needs—checks accompanied letters of encouragement, groceries were provided; Mark Mauldin, a Christian garage mechanic who repaired our car's brakes, had even given us a month to pay him.

Returning from the store one afternoon, we spotted a white police car parked in front of our home. Our hearts pounded as we pulled into the driveway and rushed into the house. Sitting on the living room couch were my sister and mother, with a weeping Pamela in between. A uniformed officer was standing in front of them, lecturing Pam.

"What's going on here?" I asked, trying not to sound upset.

The patrolman whipped around and, seeing me, smiled, "Oh, good afternoon, sir. Are you her father?"

"Yes."

"Well, I'm sorry, but there's been a little accident. I was just trying to impress upon your daughter that she should be a lot more careful about riding her bicycle. She rode right into a car at the bottom of the hill and was knocked off the bike. I think she's okay. She's more scared than anything."

The officer coughed nervously and started toward the door. "Well, I guess my job's done . . . ."

After he left, we checked Pam carefully for bruises and scratches. She had scraped her thigh. While it wasn't serious, we decided to take her to the hospital for a check up. In our situation we had to take extra precautions for our children's welfare.

On the way, Pamela was worried. She had severely scratched the woman's car and realized that we couldn't afford to pay for the damage. She also feared that any problem at home could separate the family again.

"Gee, Daddy," she cried, "I got into trouble with the police—will they take us away?"

I didn't know what to say about that, but tried to reassure her. "Honey, the devil has intended harm for you. He probably wanted to kill you—but the Lord didn't allow that."

As she looked up at me, her sobs subsided.

"You know what it says in Romans 8:28?" I smiled cheerfully.

Pam shook her head.

"It says that all things work together for good. Know what that means?"

"No."

"It means that the Lord is going to take this situation and turn it around for *our* good. Don't be afraid. The Lord will work things out."

While Pam was being examined, I called our insurance agent. Sure enough, the accident was covered by our house policy. Pam was relieved, perhaps even more than I, at the news.

As we pulled up to our house, she anxiously pointed to a sedan parked in front.

"Dad—that's the car I hit."

The owner was having a friendly chat with my mother and sister in the living room when Pam, Lucky, and I walked into the house. Concerned about our daughter, Earnestine, "Ernie" Rojas had stopped by to see if she was all right.

"I called my agent, and our insurance will take care of the damage," I reported after the initial greetings.

"I'm not concerned about that, just your daughter," she responded defensively.

Pamela's accident sparked a number of blessings. While Lucky and I were at our trial in San Bernardino the next two weeks, some friends of the Rojas' gave us sixty dollars worth of groceries, just when my mother and sister were at their wit's ends wondering where the next day's meals were coming from. When our air cooling system broke, Ernie's husband Dick, a plumber, fixed it without charge. On the weekends, the whole family was brimming with joyful reports of what God had done through the Rojas family and their friends. But another blessing was still to come.

I was sitting at our dining room table, feeling frustrated over the brake repair debt. I was just about to call Mark and tell him that we couldn't pay when I heard a knock at the front door. It was Dick.

"Hi, Dick! Come on in. Hey, thanks a lot for fixing our cooler!"

He shrugged as if it were nothing and walked in.

"Won't you sit down?" I offered, motioning toward the dining room table.

"Thank you. I can only stay a minute. I just wanted to drop this off . . ." He handed me an envelope. ". . . This is the check we received from your insurance company to fix our car, but for some reason . . . well, we just can't cash it—I don't feel this money belongs to me. Ernie and I agreed that it should go to you."

"W-well, thank you, Dick," I stammered. "I really appreciate this." I stared at the envelope in my hand. "We definitely could use the money . . . thank you."

Dick shrugged again. "That's okay," he smiled. "I've gotta go now."

After he left, I ripped open the envelope and looked at the check. I gasped at the amount—just a few cents more than my bill for the brakes.

The family came running at my excited shouts, "Praise the Lord!"

"See?" I crowed. "Look at the bill and then the check Dick Rojas just gave me." I held both up for all to see. "Remember, Pam, what I said about Romans 8:28? See—it's true!" She nodded happily. "God has taken that accident and blessed us many times. He has taken what Satan intended for harm and turned it around for our good."

I thank the Lord for giving my family such an outstanding lesson.

How I got my job back at Goldstone is another miracle. After the trial, I again applied there for employment. My chances for reinstatement were next to impossible, but the Bendix Corporation, which runs

Goldstone, promised to consult its corporate offices and lawyers on the east coast. Because of the unusual circumstances in my case, they would have to decide. Their long-awaited decision was welcome news. They would not only rehire me, but would restore my seniority. It was as though I had never been terminated. Today, several years later, I'm still working there and have been promoted to a supervisory position.

Still another provision of God's love and grace was our return to Calvary Christian Center. Feeling unwelcome there, we had worshiped elsewhere hoping time would heal bitter hearts. Occasionally, we would visit the church, and one day Pastor Nash expressed his love for us publicly. During Sunday school that morning, I spoke of the need to encourage and pray for our pastor.

Gradually we were accepted back into fellowship. Today we are once again members of Calvary Christian Center. I substitute for Pastor Nash when he cannot teach his Bible class and am a member of the board of deacons. We are experiencing love and unity in the church and thank God that we can be a part of it.

After our conviction, the reaction of the people in the community toward us was mixed. The NASA director at Goldstone welcomed me back warmly. Lucky and I had suffered enough, he reasoned. Some of the men would not speak to me at first, but warmed up when I continued to show them the love of God. One man to this day will not speak—only glare. Like some in town, his bitterness still runs hard and deep.

Occasionally, neighborhood children will talk with our kids about Wesley's death. Just last summer Jay asked his mother one day, "Mom, how did Wesley die?" We wondered if that question had been prompted by something his friends had said. Sometimes Lucky and I catch people in town looking askance at us.

Lucky is still self-conscious in stores. For a long time after the trial, she was fearful of signing her name on a check at the store. A supermarket clerk recently exclaimed, "*You're* Alice Parker?" Lucky couldn't help wonder, *Is the clerk thinking, "she's the one?"* Although we have found general acceptance in Barstow, living here has made us sensitive to our actions—especially in disciplining the children.

Spanking became very difficult. A crying child of parents convicted of felony child abuse can mean only one thing to a vindictive public. We lived in constant fear of a neighbor calling the police. What if they found a hand mark or red welt on our children? Would the police take them away? We had to move very carefully in the glass house that we had made for ourselves.

During those years, our family went through the motions of normal life. Yet someone dear and precious was gone. Time is a good healer of wounds, but the loss of Wesley was an amputation. An amputee can walk around on his artificial leg seemingly with little difficulty, but he is ever aware that a part of him is missing.

Sometimes around the dinner table the pain would become nearly unbearable. In her mind Lucky would imagine Wesley's responses to the children's chatter. Looking at his empty chair in silent agony, her tears could not flow because the stream of hurt ran too deeply.

At times when satellites were not whizzing through space above the tracking station, I would take short walks under the stars. Strolling along a dark road and up a slight hill, I would gaze longingly into the sky feeling the agony of David in the Bible when he cried, "Absolom, Absolom. My son, Absolom!" Then, unable to bear the pain any longer, I would stop and weep, "Wesley, Wesley, my son . . . Lord, tell Wesley I love him. Tell Wesley I'm sorry."

Somehow in the loneliness of my loss, I found comfort. It seemed that the Lord had answered, that He had called Wesley to His side and said, "Wess, your dad wants you to know that he still loves you."

Perhaps this accounts for a dream Lucky experienced not long ago: It was dusk and she was sitting in the dining room talking with Pat. Suddenly, there was a loud explosion, and the wind blew harder than any she had witnessed on the desert. The large tree in our front yard was blowing violently. She stood in surprise, the earth shaking beneath her feet. I ran out of our bedroom to see if she and Pat were all right.

Jay began to cry from his bedroom, and Lucky rushed to his room, took him in her arms, and tried to bring comfort amid our quaking house. He looked toward his bedroom doorway and pointed, mouth agape. Lucky turned and, much to her surprise, there stood Wesley, grinning like a kid who had just played a big joke on his mom. He was enjoying the element of surprise.

Still holding Jay, Lucky rushed to embrace Wess. The three of them stood there, hugging each other. Perfect peace replaced the panic of the earthquake, violent wind and explosion. At that moment, Lucky knew there was no need to ask Wesley's forgiveness. He understood, and perfect communication, harmony, and forgiveness flowed between them. All the pain, sorrow, and remorse melted away in that moment. It was just as though Wesley had not suffered and died.

Through this little touch of Heaven in a dream, we have taken much comfort. I can now understand God's wisdom in not bringing Wesley back in answer to our agonizing prayers. We have committed our son into His care, confident that our family will be reunited one day. Sometimes we have wondered whether anyone can understand the trial we've gone through. Only the Lord can. Yet it was not by our strength that we survived. We are no stronger than the person who's experienced a lesser ordeal. God gave us the grace to endure and triumph.

Recalling the judge's willingness to terminate our probation, I contacted our probation officer to make the necessary recommendation to ask that our felony conviction be reduced to misdemeanors. Judge Williams responded favorably. A date and time were set for another court appearance, and Lucky and I waited patiently as the gears of justice began to crank and groan into action.

The day finally arrived. It was still quite early as we drove down the Cajon Pass into San Bernardino. The smog of the summer day had yet to become oppressive. Hopeful that the judge would reduce our felony to a misdemeanor, I was confident that he would terminate our probation.

I parked our car in the lot across the street from the County Courthouse, and we walked briskly toward the massive building. How different this court appearance was from our first day of trial. Lucky was calm, not frightened as she had been that day. As we drew nearer, I looked up again to the judge's chambers, and jury deliberation room of Department Ten. I remembered the faces of the jurors peering out, the heated arguments, the pain Lucky and I suffered at the hands of the prosecutor. At least *that* was over.

Again we plunged into the bustling halls of justice—employees scurrying to work, some waiting impatiently for the slow elevators. Suddenly, we were herded into the confines of one elevator for the ride to the third floor. Lucky and I stepped out into . . . silence. Gone were the lights, cameras, and hurried questions by reporters. We walked hand in hand into the courtroom.

Bill Russler was waiting for us. We sat down with him at the Counselor's table. The courtroom scene hadn't changed much from our trial, except that the prosecutor's chair and jury box were empty. A lone court watcher was in the gallery. What a relief it was to sit—just us three—at the table. Alone. The atmosphere was casual, relaxed.

Judge Williams finally emerged from his private entry, stepped up to the bench and sat down. He was as I remembered him, possessing the quiet, strong dignity of a ruling patriarch.

"The court is now in session," the bailiff intoned.

As the judge ruled on our case, my heart thumped excitedly at the stirring words he spoke: ". . . and so, in the light of the probation officer's recommendation and his report of their exemplary lives, I have ruled to not only terminate sentence and reduce the convictions from felony to misdemeanor, but to overturn the convictions from guilty to not guilty . . . ."

Conviction overturned! Lucky and I were *innocent*.

Innocent of all charges! Caught in the whirl of this sudden event, I stood to accept the judge's generous decision.

"May I say something, Your Honor?"

"Yes."

"Your Honor, I . . . I appreciate your fairness in this matter," I stammered, searching for words to say. "My wife and I are very grateful . . . thank you for your understanding these last four years, and for all that you've done for us."

I sat down abruptly as the judge nodded. He rose, left the room, and the bailiff dismissed the court. It all happened so fast that Lucky and I were stunned. Bill congratulated us with a broad grin and handshakes as a reporter hastily left the gallery to phone in his story. We were relieved and happy at the ruling. This was a turning point, a visual aid revealing just the first step in what God would do to transform our ordeal into something good. At this we could rejoice.

Still, the somber shroud of Wesley's absence hung above us.

The hall was empty. Bill had followed the reporter out of the courtroom, and we were in the corridor alone—in bold contrast to the days of the trial. We walked hand in hand toward the elevators. Four years ago our lawyers had strongly urged us to appeal the conviction. But the Lord accomplished the same thing without the pain of another long, drawn-out trial.

We met the judge at the elevators. This was one of the few times I had seen him outside the courtroom as a man and not a magistrate. We exchanged greetings and shook hands as the "down" elevator doors opened.

"By the way, I've developed diabetes since your case was in court," he said solemnly. "It's sort of ironic, isn't it? I better understand what you two went through with your boy, especially now that I have a closer association with the disease."

He gave a fatherly wave and stepped down the hall and through another door.

As we entered our elevator, I pushed the button for the ground floor and we started our short, silent descent. The judge's words saddened me. Lucky took my hand and squeezed it, taking my mind off of him.

"Let's go celebrate tonight," she smiled. "Let's tell Lois Brown and Larry Montoya the good news."

I brightened at the mention of our friends.

As we stepped toward the double glass doors of the back entrance, I thought of the significance of the judge's decision and of the Lord's work in our lives.

We were free.

Free from the bondage of guilt and shame that had tormented us through our ordeal. Free from the stigma of our felony convictions. Free to grow into a new abundant life of Christian maturity and balance.

Lucky squeezed my hand again as we strode through the warm sunshine toward our car.

"This is just the beginning, honey."